CONTENTS

Credits

Editor: Catherine Butcher

Commissioning team: Roy Crowne, Andy Frost, Laurence Singlehurst

Production: Hannah Talbot

Additional material: Caroline Kimber

Design: www.danielwatsondesign.co.uk

Published by: HOPE and Share Jesus International in Partnership with Crossing London

HOPE and Share Jesus International are registered charities: HOPE (1116005) Share Jesus International (1089784)

ISBN: 978-0-9567038-2-8

INTRODUCTION
BECOMING CONFID

Andy Frost
Mission Director of Crossing London and Director of Share Jesus International

Roy Crowne
Executive Director of HOPE

I am frequently amazed at the representation the historical Jesus gets in our culture. Hours of airtime, hundreds of pages in the press, plus masses of internet coverage and films are devoted to the historical Jesus – especially at key moments in the Christian calendar like Christmas and Easter. To have conversations about Jesus seems totally acceptable. The challenge is to shift from the historical to the personal. It's then that lives can be touched through one-to-one conversations; it's then that we discover that Jesus still has the ability to transform lives, families and communities.

When Peter wrote to the early church he said: 'Always be prepared to give an answer to everyone who asks you to give the reason for the hope that you have. But do this with gentleness and respect...' (1 Peter 3:15). The challenge remains the same for us today.

The Archbishop of Canterbury Justin Welby has set out a vision for the church where 'it is the role of every member of the church of Jesus Christ to bear witness to their faith; to say "I know Jesus Christ and I want to introduce you to him".'

This vision is of a church, where each of us is confident to put our faith into words. That's the aim of this resource. As always, prayer is the starting point. We need to co-operate with God's Holy Spirit, listening well to God and to the people we are with, so we can speak appropriately at the right time.

What contemporary and relevant metaphors can we use to share the gospel? We clearly have a mandate to communicate, but often we don't communicate well, because we use the wrong words, the wrong emphasis, or we resort to Christian jargon. This book aims to help you to find the right words and the right context to share the hope you have because of Jesus.

And so we pray that together, with the Holy Spirit helping us, we will become effective witnesses to the Jesus who can transform anyone's life and anyone's situation.

Roy Crowne
Executive Director, HOPE

WHAT'S THE CONTEXT?

Laurence Singlehurst on the call to share the gospel

Jesus said, 'All authority in heaven and on earth has been given to me. Therefore go and make disciples of all nations…' Matthew 28:18-19.

Where are we in the great challenge of sharing the gospel? Over the last 30 years much has been achieved. There are vibrant expressions of local church in every denomination up and down the country. We have learned that the gospel must be shared in word and action, and over the last 20 years there has been a huge increase in the number of projects where the church has gone out to love its community unconditionally. Churches have recognised that we can't just wait in our church buildings for people to turn up. Slowly but surely, we have picked up the 'go' message of Matthew 28, and a new holistic missional emphasis is creeping through the church. This can be seen in the work of Fresh Expressions, Mark Greene's work at the London Institute for Contemporary Christianity and through others who have understood the importance of equipping and empowering individuals to be witnesses to Jesus wherever they may be, be that in an office or at the school gate.

However, a significant and difficult challenge still presents itself to us, which has prompted this book. With all this endeavour and good work, having expressed love and built relationships, we often slip back into default mode and speak in language that makes very little sense to those outside the church. It is important for us to understand what has taken place historically and what words, metaphors and connection points we can use to communicate the gospel effectively in contemporary society.

So what has happened historically? Around the 1730s what is sometimes called The Great Awakening created an extraordinary movement of lay people who weren't chained to church buildings or old ways of expressing faith. They preached in the open air and sang new songs with contemporary tunes. In the 1800s this movement had a super boost from the growth of Sunday schools. Christian philanthropists recognised that children working in Britain's factories were growing up illiterate. Sunday was the only day they weren't at work so Sunday schools were started and by 1825, 1.25 million children attended. By 1870, 75% of all children were going to Sunday school, learning to read and write, as well as learning Christian values. As a result, at the beginning of the 20th century, we were a nation with a strong Christian moral framework and high church attendance which slowly declined after the First World War. Even in the 1950s, when Billy Graham spoke so powerfully, the language of sin, being born again, the need to repent, and the emphasis on forgiveness still made sense to unchurched people.

However, today's culture is very different. Our postmodern nation no longer has the same Christian moral framework. Less than 3% of children go to Sunday school; church attendance is less than 10% and the majority of our population have very little biblical literacy: words like 'sin', 'repent', 'born again', 'saved', 'Jesus is Lord' for example, make very little sense. The offer of forgiveness can seem pointless because individuals have no sense that they have done anything wrong.

So the challenge of the parable of the sower is before us. It is clear from this parable that the bad soil represents those people who do not understand the Christian message - it is not enough just to hear the words, they must also be understood by the hearer. Also, we must get the balance right between the costs and benefits of the gospel otherwise we have 'rocky soil' converts who love the benefits, but don't understand the cost and fall away. I think we now understand that the preaching of the '80s and '90s may have oversold the benefits, consumerised the gospel message and reaped ourselves a problem.

The good soil is people who understand. They understand the good news, and they also understand the implications of embracing that good news: that in their surrender to Christ they are embracing a new value system, a new way to live.

In this book we are seeking to put forward ideas and examples that help us face this challenge. Just as Jesus did, we need to translate gospel truth into language understood by our culture. As we contextualise the gospel and experiment with different images, metaphors and language, we need to embrace failure as our friend. When we seek to communicate and fail, we need to ask ourselves what can be learnt from this experience and try again. Then we will quickly acquire a huge amount of good practice and learn from one another what works in which context and what language is really powerful. The challenge of contextualisation is two-fold: it is to share the gospel in words and actions that people understand without watering down its content; and to have a relevant expression of church that can nurture those who respond.

Laurence Singlehurst speaks regularly at major events, conferences and churches. He worked in Youth with a Mission from 1976 to 2003 and as National Director from 1990 to 2003. He is author of Sowing Reaping Keeping (IVP) and The Gospel Message Today – Language that Connects in Communicating the Gospel (Grove) and is currently Director of Cell UK, and a member of the HOPE leadership team.

NATURALLY SUPERNATURAL

Live a holy life, without living in a hole! says Roy Crowne

Sharing our faith is both immensely practical and natural, but also has an element of the supernatural. There are certain things we can learn about sharing faith – you'll find many in this resource, but we've also been given another helper, the Holy Spirit, who enables us to be naturally supernatural.

There are two key things to remember as we share our faith: the first is lifestyle. I Peter 3:15 says that we need to acknowledge Jesus as our Lord. Jesus' Lordship should affect our relationships, family, money, work and every aspect of our life so that we live a distinctive life; a life that will provoke questions about why we do what we do. To live differently is to live a holy life (1 Peter 1:15) but without living in a hole!

That means we will have a lifestyle that becomes attractive: 'to shine like stars in a dark world' (Philippians 2:15). But that is not the whole piece. The second thing to remember is that the Holy Spirit intervenes supernaturally in what we do; effective faith-sharing needs both.

Roy Crowne is Executive Director of HOPE. He was National Director of Youth for Christ in Britain for 12 years.

THE HOLY SPIRIT'S WORK

Pastor Mo looks at what the Bible tells us about the Holy Spirit's work

The Holy Spirit's ministry is revealed by Jesus in John 16:8-14. Jesus described the ministry of the Holy Spirit as follows:

1. to prove the world to be in the wrong about sin and righteousness and judgement
2. to guide believers into all truth,
3. and in doing all these things, he will glorify the Lord Jesus Christ.

Christ's post-resurrection mandate to his disciples states that they 'will receive power when the Holy Spirit comes on you; and you will be my witnesses in Jerusalem, and in all Judea and Samaria, and to the ends of the earth' (Acts 1:8).

The Holy Spirit empowers Christians to proclaim the limitless riches of Christ to the unsaved. The ministry of the Holy Spirit as outlined in John 16:8 is to convict people of sin, of righteousness and judgement.

However, human agency is important as exemplified by Paul in Romans 10:14-15: 'How, then, can they call on the one they have not believed in? And how can they believe in the one of whom they have not heard? And how can they hear without someone preaching to them? And how can anyone preach unless they are sent? As it is written: "How beautiful are the feet of those who bring good news!"'

Witnessing or evangelising is working with the Holy Spirit who convicts sinners and brings them to acknowledge the saving grace of Christ. All Christians are expected to be involved in evangelism or mission (Matthew 28:18-20) but the Holy Spirit can have specific tasks for Christians in the eternal purpose of God, as he did for Paul and Barnabas (Acts 13:2).

Pastor Modupe Afolabi is the Executive Administrator of the Redeemed Christian Church of God (RCCG) Central Office in the UK.

LIGHT'S COMING

You won't convince anyone, but the Holy Spirit can, says Roger Forster

Most people want to live and live well. However, for most people living well means a luxury home, a footballer's wages, cars, boats, holidays and 'things' ad infinitum. Even those of us who would like others and in our own personal good.

content would confess we could always do with 'a little bit more'. We never have quite enough. It is well documented how both the rich and the poor always think they are missing out somewhere. Much of our conversation is about this dissatisfaction, and it provides a continuous opportunity to lovingly speak of Jesus. He has come that we might live life to its full (John 10:10)

Many will deny that they are less than content, but this should not divert us. Philosophers have named this feeling of inadequacy and lost-ness, ache and even guilt as the 'God-shaped blank' inside all humans. I remember, when I was a young Christian, how surprised I was upon talking with a student for over an hour while he declared he was an atheist and had no needs. Suddenly he looked straight in my eyes and said: 'Alright then, I need Jesus don't I? Let's pray.'

Five essentials for evangelism

When you share Jesus, as Jesus commands, he also promised 1 the Holy Spirit will also share with you both (John 16:25-27). You are not able to convince anyone, but the Holy Spirit can (John 16:9-11). When someone says 'How do you know Jesus died for me, it was 2000 years ago and you weren't there?' The Spirit says 'No he wasn't, but I was.'

Very early in my Christian life when trying to win people to Christ, I learned two important points I have never lost. Dave, a very aggressive and destructive gang leader, had come to our youth group a few times but never listened. In fact he would always finish up trashing the room. One night he was quiet. My brother said 'Why don't you talk to Dave?' I nervously replied 'Why don't you?' but I did what my elder brother demanded.

Dave began: 'I'm an atheist and I have no needs. I have all I want in life'. After an hour and a half or so he said 'I'm still an atheist'. I didn't think I was doing too well, but said 'Why don't you tell God you are an atheist?' He said 'That's stupid'. I replied 'No it's not. If he is not there you haven't lost anything and that's the way to find out if anyone is around, you call out for them' (Romans 10:13).

'Alright' he replied 'I will'. Now I was worried and prayed a rather half-hearted prayer with him. Dave then prayed 'Lord if you are there I want to believe in you' then he added 'and do your will'. He looked up and to my amazement

he smiled saying 'I think the light's coming.' Now I didn't go around Peckham and South East London saying 'Have you seen the light?' Two days later he gave his life to Christ.

When we are seeking to bring people to Jesus we need two more essentials for responses to God. 2 An act of the will to do God's will, that is repentance. 3 An act of welcoming, believing, or trusting Christ (John 1:12; Acts 20:21). If one or other of these two elements is missing it may be the reason why some folk respond with 'It didn't work'.

I had also to learn a further lesson. It is God who does the supernatural birth and not my less than efficient attempts at spiritual midwifery. So 4 our prayer before, during and after helping someone to come through to Christ is essential as it gives room to the Spirit to enlighten. Encourage that person to pray also, even if they think they can't.

One other factor in sharing Jesus with anyone is 5 faith. Our confidence is in the lovely message we have to tell of the life, death and resurrection of Jesus together with our dependence on the Holy Spirit with whom we work by faith. After my conversion a handful of friends became Christians and then conversions stopped although I was trying hard to win folk. I complained to the Lord 'You said "come after me and I will make you fishers of men" (Mark 1:17) but it is not happening.'

It was as though I was fishing by dropping bricks on the fish, I missed and they fled. The Lord said to me 'I said I will make you a fisher of others. Trust me!'

Thank you Lord; that takes the fear and strain away. Listen to his word and speak it! Good fishing.

Roger Forster is the founder of Ichthus Christian Fellowship, Vice President of Tearfund and a former Chairman of the Evangelical Alliance.

CALENDAR MOMENTS

The church's calendar offers a rhythm of mission, says Catherine Butcher

Is your church known for its irresistibly infectious joy? We have so much to celebrate and the people in our communities deserve a welcome at the party!

Christmas and Easter are traditional times for nominally-Christian people to attend church. Make sure they leave asking questions prompted by overwhelmingly generous hospitality, our loving care for one another as Christian brothers and sisters, and by our warm welcome – as well as being inspired by what they have heard, said or sung. Sharing a mince pie and coffee after the service could be more significant than the sermon for your guests – that's the time to talk about what Jesus means in our daily lives.

The church's calendar offers a rhythm of mission as you reach out to neighbours, colleagues and friends: as well as Christmas and Easter, how about a party at Pentecost or a special supper to celebrate harvest? Each of these Christian festivals can be a season to 'sow seeds' - to prompt questions about big issues like – Who am I? What am I here for? Where am I going in life?

Make sure that the next step is easy for people to take: at each guest event publicise the date of the next special event and dates of any event or course where people can explore the Christian gospel for the first time.

I like to think of my home and church as embassies of heaven. When guests are invited to an embassy they receive the very best hospitality – a taste of the country they have not yet visited that makes them want to visit for themselves.

An embassy is also there to help in a crisis. As well as welcoming people from our communities to celebrate key moments in the Christian calendar, we are also available to serve, support and care at life's most difficult times. On Remembrance Day, and if there is a crisis in the community, people turn to the church to take a lead in ceremonies. In the midst of the rituals of grief and remembering, let's be people who take every opportunity to talk, sensitively, about the hope we have because of Jesus.

HOPE's Communications Director Catherine Butcher, was founding editor of Families First magazine for Mothers' Union. She is on the PCC of St John's Meads, Eastbourne.

CHANGING LIVES

God can use you to reach out to your neighbours, says Rebekah Brettle

Change comes to all of us. Sometimes rapid changes leave us feeling vulnerable, even when change is for the better, such as a wedding, a new baby or a new home. Also changes in people's lives can prompt questions about faith, and offer opportunities for us to show the love of Jesus. The street where you live is full of people experiencing change. It is no accident that you live where you do. God can use you to reach out to your neighbours with actions and words!

The Neighbourhood Prayer Network aims to see every street in the UK covered in Christian prayer, with people praying for, caring for and sharing their faith with their neighbours. Ask your neighbours if they have any specific prayer needs (prayer requests should be kept confidential) and pray for them by name, looking out for opportunities to serve them.

A new baby, a new job, a wedding, retirement, illness in the family or bereavement – each of life's changes offer an opportunity for you to show Jesus' love in simple, practical ways and to talk about what Jesus means to you.

New Baby

- Many new parents are exhausted and want to be left alone, but make them aware that if they want help, you are available.
- Let them know about Parent and Toddler groups, parenting courses or other practical help available in your church and surrounding churches.
- Invite new fathers to your local men's breakfast.

New Job

- Send a 'congratulations on your new job' card.
- If you have a testimony about how God has helped you in a new job, ask God to give you opportunity to share this.

Wedding

- Give your neighbour a wedding card/gift.
- Ask if there is any practical help needed in the lead up to the wedding.
- If you are invited to the wedding, attend, even if it is not a church-based or traditional wedding, but don't be offended if you're not invited!
- Invite the new couple for a meal or a coffee a few months after the wedding.

Retirement

- Buy your neighbour a retirement card or a small gift.
- Most people who have just retired don't see themselves as old, so an invitation to the OAPs' lunch club might not go down too well! If your church has a walking group or activity groups, this might be an opportunity to invite them along.

Pain

- Emotional or physical pain can cause different reactions in people; some want to be left alone; others are more than happy for companionship, visits and friendship.

- Offer to go shopping, cook a meal or take them to doctors' appointments.

- If they are admitted to hospital, visit them.

- Be there to listen.

- If you have a testimony of how God has helped you through a painful experience, ask God for the opportunity to share your story with your neighbour.

- Wait for your neighbour to ask you questions about your faith and be willing to answer them.

- Tell your neighbour that you are praying for them.

Bereavement

People grieve in different ways. Some people don't seem upset at the time, only to be hit with grief several weeks or months later; others are overwhelmed with grief. Some people deal with grief by being angry towards others. If you're on the receiving end of this - don't take it personally; use this as a cue to hold your neighbour up in prayer. Some people are glad of company; others want to be left alone. Please respect your neighbour's wishes. When people are faced with death, they often ask spiritual questions; wait for your neighbour to bring this up.

- Send a bereavement card and some flowers.

- Offer practical help before or after the funeral.

- Check with your neighbour if they would like you to attend the funeral.

- Offer to provide meals.

- If your church offers bereavement counselling, let your neighbour know about it.

A former GP, Rebekah Brettle works for the Neighbourhood Prayer Network.
www.neighbourhoodprayer.net

BEING A GOOD NEIGHBOUR

We moved into our new home four years ago. From the outset, we wanted to be fairly low-key as far as being followers of Jesus was concerned, wanting to get to know our neighbours and for them to get to know us as 'normal' people first, rather than have them put us in a 'religious' box. As we were all moving into a new-build estate, we were all new together, so it was a good time to start new things and try to create community.

First I started a neighbourhood watch scheme, working with another neighbour, which has now expanded to the whole estate. This provides a great opportunity to get to know people by name.

I took a card and plant to every new neighbour as they moved in to the houses that were still being built. I organised our first street party in August 2008, again just for immediate neighbours, which was followed by a Big Lunch in 2009 and 2010 for the whole estate.

Every Christmas we have neighbourhood carols on our driveway with mulled wine and mince pies. I take a card to each new baby that I find out about and/or weddings etc and I regularly prayer-walk the estate, praying for households by name. I keep a prayer book and write down significant conversations, and I pray for the right moment to let each of my neighbours know that I pray for them. I have told about a dozen so far.

It's nothing spectacular, and I'm not sure where it will lead, but I just keep chipping away, praying for them all and slowly becoming the neighbour that everyone knows and trusts.

A Neighbourhood Prayer Network member

REACHING A MISSING GENERATION

Kiera Phyo highlights the challenges of reaching 18-30s

We sang 'I wanna be a history maker' and believed we were part of an army, a generation that could change the world. We were inspired to shift culture, to be shapers, not shaped. We were hastening the day of Jesus' return...And we're left wondering whether we should still be hoping for revival.

Once, we were totally committed to the church youth group and to Christ; ten years later and we are nowhere to be seen in church - yours or anyone else's. We are part of a dramatic decline in church attendance. (The numbers attending church in the 20-29 age group declined from 520,900 in 1985 to 230,600 in 2005, a decline of 62%, according to the Evangelical Alliance 'Missing Generation?' report.)

We are part of a culture and a society that says... 'I shop therefore I am'. We are propelled to consume...our identities formed not just by the chosen brands adorning us, but by the practice of commodification. We have idolised self and, like making an offering to a god, our consumer habits supply the sacred goods we bring ourselves.

The digital world augments our every day. We are able to shoot films, make documentaries, publish articles, tell our story with an instagram-picture-perfect lens. There's a big platform open to us; we have the tools to speak loudly and, with the right content, the potential to be heard - to build community, to gather followers, to create something, to start something.

Leaders can look unlikely. We are empowered. In Andy Crouch's words, 'the most informal and anti-institutional demographic cohort in a century, Generation X, moved uneasily and unsteadily into adulthood,' and 'The most powerful CEO in America was universally known as "Steve".'

Information is fast and shared. Wikipedia's 26 million articles are written by volunteers. Ted Talks, Twitter, YouTube - we eat information and are motivated to contribute. (Thank you Tim Berners-Lee for setting an online value of sharing.)

Collaboration is celebrated.

Key questions

There are two questions to consider when thinking about communicating the gospel to this audience: what is the story and who is the story- teller?

What understanding and experience of the gospel do 18-30s currently have? Not much. This group does not regularly attend church or have parents that do (20% of under 20 year olds have never attended church). We are talking to a group of people with little religious experience.

Three images my generation has of the gospel (by no means a summation):

1. It is intolerant

With little church affiliation, media is a prominent access point and opinion-former for the public. The debates about women bishops and same-sex marriage are the height of some people's experience of the gospel. A message that implies, depending on who you are, Christianity will not wholly embrace you. When this generation believes tolerance is king, and considers it a civic duty, these are reason enough to discount the Jesus message.

2. It is disconnected

The gospel has failed to be communicated in a meaningful way. The strange man shouting about hell on the street comes to mind. As my unchurched friend recently said when he attended a Sunday service with me, 'The singing was like intense rock karaoke about a guy's blood. All that was missing was the ball that bounced from word to word.' The language of sin, repentance, blood, born again, salvation, are foreign words failing to resonate, leaving this generation feeling 'the gospel has little to do with my life.'

3. It didn't look after me. (Especially relevant to the churched missing generation who've 'left the building').

Did 'Salvation go on Sale'? Did the competitive nature for business to offer better, cheaper products wangle its way into our theology? Did we 'lower the price of salvation', appealing to our consumer-customer?

Was the gospel sold as life insurance: if we follow Jesus, life won't hurt us, we are protected? And our perception of a heavenly Father became more like Father Christmas; if we hold up our end, we will get good presents.

In this story, Jesus ends up owing us stuff: happiness, a good life, avoidance of pain, never feeling alone, direction on what to do, who to marry, where to study. So when life goes wrong and pain is present, the consumer returns the product: 'This gospel, is not the one I ordered.'

Who is the story-teller?

Who should be the story-teller to this generation? A couple of years ago Tearfund surveyed 500 young people and young adults. We found, when it came to being motivated for action, peers matter.

Alongside their church leader, 17-25-year-olds were most inspired for action by their peers. We realised people in this demographic can, potentially, do a better job at engaging their sphere of influence than a highly-skilled and experienced employee. And we've been facilitating this since then.

Judith Rich Harris in *The Nurture Assumption* (Bloomsbury) emphasises the influence groups of peers have on one another:

'The changers of cultures are people in their teens or early twenties who have an age group of their own. Groupness motivates them to be different from the generation of their parents and teacher....They are so anxious to contrast themselves with the generation ahead of them that the differences don't even have to be improvement....They adopt different behaviours and different philosophies; they invent new words and new forms of adornment. When you put together a group of people who are not children and not adults, what you have is a mechanism for rapid social change' (p275).

The power of the peer is able to do something other people cannot. They don't need to adapt their language, break into the group, be culturally relevant, etc. The peer is part of the group, authentic by nature. In a culture seeking authentic connection, wanting to participate in a collaborative journey, recognising informal leaders; the peer is the powerful story-teller. For a demographic that is empowered digitally to speak, vocalise and lead, how are we empowering this generation to lead our story-telling?

What hope is there for 18s-30s?

How do we share the powerful message of Jesus with 18s-30s? What story, truth, metaphor, image resonates? Here are some ideas.

The gospel is...

1. A Story of Inclusion

Following a Rabbi was the first century version of attending Oxbridge; gathering the scholarly and the best. Then a different kind of Rabbi arrived inviting the ordinary, uneducated, average to follow him. After three years, they graduated, becoming a group of people who broke down barriers of marginalisation and who shocked society with a radical pursuit of welcoming anybody.

2. A Story of Wonder

At the end of my sister's wedding service I was with her school mates (none of them familiar with church) when a guy came up to my dad and said 'What happened when we were singing and how can I have more of that?' When society has let go of a meta-narrative, everyone has the right to their own truth, and apologetics fall short, maybe we need an encounter with Jesus.

3. A Story of Collaboration

God is not Harry Potter. He is not a magician and doesn't have a magic wand to make the world a better place. Instead of maneuvering pawns, God chose to work with us to be his hands and feet.

God invites us to host heaven on earth.

4. A Story of Justice

Jesus was a revolutionary. Not just meek and mild, but politically engaged, standing up for the oppressed, defending the rights of the poor.

5. A Story of the Earth

Genesis 1-3. God created the cosmos and everything in it. God shared Jesus with the world, letting us know it is a good place to be. God invites us to work together with him and each other, to care for creation and make the world a good home.

6. A Story of Equality

God made everyone in his image. Every person matters.

7. A Story of Friendship

God is not controlling, but a companion. He doesn't offer an easy ride, but he says 'I will be with you. You are not alone.'

Kiera Phyo leads Tearfund's Youth & Emerging Generation team. She is a member of the HOPE leadership team and the leadership team of her local church - Restore, Peckham.

FINDING JESUS AT THE END OF LIFE'S JOURNEY

Liz Stacey, who has devised a nine session course based on Pilgrim's Progress, *describes how one elderly lady came to know Jesus as her saviour as a result of the course*

Working with Seniors is very rewarding but sad at times — seeing lives becoming limited and painful — but wonderful to see how the Lord meets people and offers them a hope.

One dear little lady called Sarah attended the *Pilgrim's Progress* group and remembered her son did *Pilgrim's Progress* for A level. She joined in everything wholeheartedly and had some very relevant comments to make most weeks.

There are nine sessions and we held them monthly. On the final session the story ends with the characters Christian and Hopeful going through the Valley of the Shadow and coming to the end of the narrow way. We talk about old age, pain, suffering and finally death for Christian and Hopeful. There is a great river in front of them and the city of gold at the other side. Hopeful is full of hope and faith and is able to jump in and find her way across. Christian is fearful and unsure and so finds it more difficult, but with the help of Hopeful manages to reach the other side.

It is at this point in our final session that we bring in a big celebration cake with candles on it and sing the Christian song 'Come on and celebrate'. When everyone has a cup of tea and some cake someone sings from the Adrian Plass and Phil Baggaley album *City of Gold*: 'Meet me at the finish line.' The song is

about a band of weary pilgrims coming to the end of their journey – very moving. I finish the story by telling them that Christian has arrived at his destination and his journey is complete, but we are still on our journey, our pilgrimage. Then I say:

'Right now, the Lord Jesus is preparing a place for you in heaven. But he doesn't want anyone to go there if they don't want to. We all have a choice and a chance to make a decision, to go or not to go, just like Christian at the very beginning of our story. We need to let Jesus know if we want to go and be with him, and receive from him his gift of salvation and eternal life, and all the other wonderful blessings that Jesus has promised us.'

We then read the words Jesus says to us, from John 14. The Lord Jesus tells us that he is preparing a place for us and will come and bring us to be with him. I explain that he would not want anyone to come with him to heaven who didn't want to – so if they want to go and be with him they have to use the prayer of commitment, given as part of the session, to tell Jesus that they want to follow him.

The Holy Spirit's presence was very real to us in all the sessions, but particularly in this one. I believe all those who attended responded. Sarah certainly did and found great comfort from that day on.

One day, when she had become very poorly and bedridden, I was visiting and she wanted to talk about dying. She was anxious about leaving her family, but really wanted to go. We talked about the legacy of love that she had given them and how that would remain with them. I reminded her of the time we did *Pilgrim's Progress* and of the final session when we read about Jesus going to prepare a place for her. I told her not to be frightened because he would come when the time was right and take her to be with him. She asked me if that was really true, and I assured her it was, as it was written in the Bible and was what Jesus wanted her to know. She sighed deeply and said, 'Thank you for that.' She felt great peace and died not long afterwards. It was a great privilege to know that she had gone to be with Jesus.

Liz Stacey has developed an interactive study guide based on John Bunyan's Pilgrim's Progress *which she has used with some 80 and 90 year olds to help them understand more of what the Christian life is all about. The study guide is available from Liz Stacey liz@winbap.org.uk*

FORGIVEN!

PARCHE (Pastoral Action in Residential Care Homes for the Elderly) supports churches providing fellowship, comfort, Bible teaching and friendship to elderly people living in care homes.

PARCHE's founder Buddy Reeve has countless stories of lives being changed as a result of the ministry: 'One lady I met in a home was quite depressed. She was on an oxygen cylinder and I went in to talk to her in her room. She had been a Christian but told me she'd wandered away when she got married. I spoke to her briefly and told her the Lord had never stopped loving her and if she wanted to pray, he would receive her back immediately.

'She prayed there and then and asked Jesus to forgive her. For the rest of her time in that home, she would walk around from room to room carrying her oxygen cylinder and telling the other residents what had happened to her, which was absolutely brilliant.'

OFFER PRAYER

Pete Greig says most people say 'yes' if you offer to pray with them

My neighbour wanted to chat. She always wants to chat. Mentally deferring my next appointment, I took a deep breath and remembered to ask about her husband's hospital check-up. It had been worrying, she said. He was potentially facing difficult surgery. I paused, remembering the time that she'd kindly offered me a shelf-full of old astrology books because she reckons I'm 'spiritual'.

'I think you know that I'm a Christian,' I ventured. 'Would you mind if I pray for both of you over the next couple of weeks? Sounds like things are tough. Sometimes it really works.'

She looked at me intently, unusually silent. And then she whispered very quietly 'thank you' and touched my arm.

People who don't want to be preached at still want to be prayed for. They may not believe in very much, but they probably do still believe in prayer. One survey showed that a whopping 20 million adults in the UK believe in the power of prayer – way more than go to church. Nine million pray daily. The percentages are much higher in America and globally, of course, the vast majority believe in prayer. In Dubai there's a prayer room on almost every corner. So offering to pray for somebody can be a brilliant way of bringing Jesus into a conversation. They will almost always appreciate your kindness and respect the depth of your faith, whether or not they share it.

By offering to pray you tell someone three important things: that you care about them, that God cares about them, and that God

can help them. It's way easier than explaining the significance of the cross, less cheesy than saying 'Jesus loves you', less terrifying than inviting them to an evangelistic meeting, more meaningful than thrusting a tract into their hand. And, of course, it only takes one miracle to change somebody's life forever. We may risk a little kudos by offering to pray, but when we don't, we risk missing out on a miraculous answer to prayer. So let me suggest seven simple keys for doing this well:

1. Be confident

It's surprisingly easy to offer to pray for somebody. Even if they don't believe it'll make any difference, they will still appreciate your kindness. I've done this for government ministers and homeless beggars and they pretty much always say 'yes, please'. Don't be freaked out if they just stare at you while you're praying - people who don't go to church don't know the etiquette. I often close my eyes when I pray for someone in the street, because it's easier to concentrate and less intense.

2. Be humble

Don't promise someone guaranteed miracles (God's not a slot machine). People appreciate your honesty if you say something like 'sometimes when I've prayed for people in the past, God's done amazing things. So it can't do any harm to try, can it?'

3. Be clear

There is an important distinction between offering to pray for someone and with them. Sometimes Christians say 'can I pray for you?', when what they really mean is, 'can I pray with you, right here and now?' It's powerful if they agree to pray with you at that moment but some people prefer to think that you will go home and quietly pray for them without any embarrassment. I was driving a lapsed Catholic home one day and suggested a quick prayer on the way. 'Please don't,' he cried. 'You need your eyes open when you're driving.' I assured him that I could chat to God with my eyes open, and he looked amazed and said 'OK'!

4. Keep it simple

No one wants to hear you yelling in tongues outside Greggs bakery, binding their spirit of fungal infection. If they're happy for you to pray with them, see if there's somewhere quiet to do so, ask before you place a hand on their arm (nowhere else) and then simply pray quietly, kindly, and quickly.

5. Be thoughtful

Make sure you pray for the person as well as the problem. What other things might you pray about? Do they have children? Are they lonely? Are there other things the Holy Spirit is whispering in your ear to pray about?

6. Be faithful

If you promise to pray for someone make sure that you really do it! And keep doing it. Jesus said that sometimes we simply have to persevere.

7. Be friendly

Wherever possible follow up the conversation. Get in touch a few days later and ask how it's going. You'll be utterly amazed at how often God does answer the prayer (He's especially keen to show his love to non-church-goers) and they will rarely tell you what's happened unless you ask. Whenever they do respond positively, take the next step and suggest a coffee or even attending an Alpha course.

Recommended resources:
www.healingonthestreets.com
www.trypraying.co.uk
www.24-7prayer.com

Pete Greig leads Emmaus Road Community Church in Guildford, writes books and serves as Director of Prayer at Holy Trinity Brompton in London. He is the founder of the 24-7 Prayer movement, which started in 1999 and has since reached more than 100 nations.

HEAR FROM GOD

Chris Frost asks 'What would Jesus like to say to the people you meet?'

More than 50% of the population in the UK are on Facebook; deep in the recesses of everybody's heart is the desire to be known. Perceiving this heart-cry, Jesus led conversations a level beyond the first century equivalent of last night's episode of *EastEnders*, by supernaturally showing people they were known.

The classic example is the story of the woman at the well, where Jesus strikes up a conversation with a request for help; 'Will you give me a drink?' (John 4:7). Imagine that, the creator of everything asking for some water! What humility!

Then the word of knowledge comes: 'The fact is, you have had five husbands, and the man you now have is not your husband' (John 4:18). Sensitively, Jesus lovingly exposes the unsatisfying idol of men resident in the woman's heart and encourages her to accept his eternally satisfying living water.

The effect of Jesus' ability to simultaneously listen to his Father and to the woman was staggering. What could have passed as every-day pleasant chit-chat, resulted in the woman bringing people from her town to Jesus, saying, 'Come, see a man who told me everything I ever did' (John 4:29). As a result 'many more became believers' (John 4:41). Truly one word of knowledge can change a town.

Sitting in a bar recently I sensed in my gut that a lady opposite had just had a close relationship breakdown. Nervously sharing that with her, she responded with: 'Who are you people? How do you know that?' She went on to explain; 'My fiancé has just split up with me. We were supposed to be getting married next week.' My friends and I were then able to explain the gospel to her in the context of Jesus wanting to be like a faithful husband to her.

Your creator speaking to you is the most natural thing in the world. He has done it and continues to do it. Next time you're talking with someone, do it like Jesus and ask him what he would like to say to them.

Chris Frost is an elder at Gateway Church Leeds (www.gatewayleeds.net) and serves as an evangelist in a wider context as part of the ChristCentral Churches Newfrontiers team.

THE GIRL IN THE RED JUMPER

Emma always dressed in black. Black summed up her feelings about herself and her life. A bizarre set of circumstances meant she had left life on the streets and was living with a family near Ashburnham Place. They had been so welcoming and forgiving, so when they gave her a gift – a bright red, woolly jumper – she couldn't refuse. And then they invited her to a Marilyn Baker concert and asked her to wear it. Marilyn is blind so it was a shock when, halfway through the evening, she stopped playing and said: 'God wants to tell the girl in the red jumper he loves her very much!' Emma jumped up and ran… God was on her case and now, more than 20 years on, Emma and her husband lead a church, introducing people to Jesus and his amazing love.

BRING HOPE

David Shosanya describes how God used him to introduce a fellow commuter to Jesus

It was rush hour and the train was crowded. Fortunately I managed to secure a seat, as did the friend I was travelling with. Two stations after boarding, the person sitting opposite us left the train and a young woman quickly sat down in the empty seat. I immediately had a strange feeling about the woman. It was a feeling I am familiar with when God is about to speak to me. I looked at my friend and he had that look in his eye that indicated 'this could be interesting'. It was.

Here's the story. The look I talked about earlier got my friend and me praying. The more we prayed the more we sensed that God wanted to do something in the situation. Conscious that we were two black men on a crowded underground train wanting to approach a young woman, we were cautious. We prayed for a few stops. Finally, when the young woman got up to leave the train we followed…

'Excuse me,' I said, 'I think that God has a message for you.' The young lady looked at us and burst out crying confessing that she had been calling out to God for help. We sat on a bench, calmed her down, shared the gospel, prayed for her, led her to Christ and referred her to a local church. An ordinary evening resulted in an individual having a personal encounter with Christ that changed her eternal destiny.

Sharing Christ in this manner is not something that is the preserve of the spiritual elite or gifted evangelist. We should not confine movements of the Spirit of God in the enterprise of sharing the gospel to the annals of church history. God is still at work today spreading the fragrance of Christ (2 Corinthians 2:14-16) in our world, within communities and to individuals that are separated from him.

Strangely, and don't ask me why, he chooses to use ordinary people, broken people, flawed people, like you and me, to show others his interest in them.

Perhaps that is the point. If God can love you and me despite our obvious faults and failings, others might also believe that he can love them too. This, I believe, is what it means to be wounded healers, a conduit of God's love and a testimony of his grace.

Yes it takes courage and we may get it wrong! So what? God appreciates our effort and works with us. Why not dare to embark on an adventure in evangelism with God and see what his grace, love and power will do in and through you as his Spirit is given permission to make God known through you to a needy world? Now over to you. Believe, act and see what God does. Go and BRING HOPE!

David Shosanya serves as a Regional Minister and Director for the London Baptist Association and is a co-founder of the Street Pastors initiative.

KNOW THE DIFFERENCE JESUS MAKES

Mark Greene's recipe for relationships that are open to the gospel

'What a lovely day,' she said, closing her eyes as she tilted her head like a giant sunflower up towards the radiant orb.

'Yes,' he replied, ' it was just like this on the day I found Jesus.'

Crowbarring an opportunity to share your testimony into a conversation is almost never the right way to develop an evangelistic relationship, particularly with people we are likely to see again. And the people we meet on our daily frontlines – in the office, at the gym, at the school gate – are usually people we are going to see again. Our goal, given that we are praying for someone and seeking their best in practical ways, is not to dump a gospel message on them but to create a relationship that is open to the gospel. And that involves developing trust.

Conversationally, there seem to me to be two keys:

1. Be open and vulnerable about who you really are – your struggles, your challenges. It creates a safe space for others.
2. Listen. Be interested in learning more about who they really are and what they are facing. Love opens ears and hearts.

You might begin with a question about how they spent the weekend, or what their favourite films or songs are – often revealing. It might be a comment about how hard things are at work, followed by a question about how they are handling it. That might naturally lead them to

ask how you are coping. Which might lead you to say, 'I hate conflict. And I nearly lost it with Mark last week so I asked a friend to pray and I'm a bit calmer. I used to have a temper that made Gordon Ramsay look like Postman Pat.'

'Really? What changed?'

Ultimately, we are seeking to communicate the difference receiving Jesus makes to our lives… and can make to theirs. Paul seems often to have given personal testimony as well as direct exposition of the gospel message (e.g. Acts 22, 26). And the more aware and grateful we are of what Jesus has done and is doing in our lives, the deeper and broader and more compelling our testimonies will be…

Pray. Love. Listen. Share. Pray.

Mark Greene is LICC's Executive Director
www. licc.org.uk

A TIME TO SPEAK...AND TO SHUT UP

God conversations are like a game of tennis, says Laurence Singlehurst

If you do a general survey of people and ask them what they think about evangelical Christians the phrase 'Bible basher' will often come up.

To my mind the first goal of any good conversation regarding faith is to leave people positive for the next Holy Spirit encounter, and the second goal is to use language and metaphors that are relevant and understandable.

So how do spiritual conversations work? Conversations are a bit like a game of tennis. A comment is made. For example, at the checkout in a shop we might be asked 'Did you have a good weekend?' I might say 'Yes, there was a very good service at my church,' which introduces a spiritual element. Now it is their turn to respond. If they hit the metaphorical tennis ball back and say 'Really, you go to church?' then I can take the conversation further, but if there is no return then I need to stop talking about spiritual things.

When people ask you questions they are giving you permission to say something. When they stop asking we need to take the hint that they don't want to hear more at this time. Leave people feeling positive about Christians

rather than continuing to talk, violating their space, or earning the title 'Bible basher'.

Laurence Singlehurst is Director of Cell UK, a member of the HOPE leadership team and the leadership of Network Church, Harpenden.

QUESTIONS FROM JENNY

Jenny, a gardener in her late 50s, is on a journey that began with God speaking to her. She helps a Christian with her garden who explains, 'Occasionally Jenny comes to do some gardening for us. One morning, she turned up unexpectedly and started weeding. I was particularly busy, but had a very loud thought: "Work alongside Jenny today." I had other plans, but I couldn't ignore that voice, so I put on the gardening gloves.

'After only a minute, the purpose of my being there became obvious. Jenny must have noticed my cross, because she asked: "Do you go to church?" She had recently been to a concert, held in a church and as she listened to the music she experienced a strange peaceful feeling, she'd never felt before. Now she wanted to find out more.

'As we worked, I told her about how I became a Christian and the change it had brought to my life. Jenny had lots of questions, so I introduced her to my midweek home group. She quickly felt like one of the family, accepted prayer and even began to pray aloud in an "if there's a God" kind of way. She is still hungry to find out more and is considering joining an Alpha course.'

GO DEEPER

Ask people how they make sense of the world, says Andy Frost

As Christians we are often on the back-foot. We are challenged to defend the reasons why we believe in Jesus. One way to take conversations deeper is to ask people how they make sense of the world. This often leads to deeper conversations.

Faith is described as '...relative certainty about matters of ultimate concern sufficient to promote action'.

At its core, faith is about three things:

1. Faith is an explanation. It is our understanding of what the world is really all about. Is our existence meaningless or is there some purpose behind why we are here?
2. Faith is confidence that our explanation of how the world works is correct.
3. Faith is action. The way we live our lives reflects the explanation that we have.

The truth is we all have faith. We all have an explanation that we are confident in, which helps us make daily decisions.

As Christians, our explanation of the world is that there is a loving God who wants us to be in relationship with him. Our confidence comes through our experience, creation, the Bible and the church. Our lives reflect this explanation in the ways we live, the prayers we pray and the way we love others.

So often as Christians we are on the back-foot. People say that our faith, our explanation, is not plausible. But perhaps it's time to challenge people on their faith or explanation of how the world works.

For example, when someone explains that they are an atheist, we could respond, 'Wow – that's incredible! I would love to know how you have such confidence that there is no God....' Or when someone says that they cannot believe in Jesus, we could ask them what they believe and then ask them to explain their reasoning.

Note that this should not be done aggressively but with love. Allow God to use you in helping others think through whether their logic really is as fool-proof as they think it is. For example, when someone explains that their faith is in science and nothing else, you could ask them if they have ever had any spiritual experiences, or whether love ever seems to be more than just a chemical reaction in the brain.

Andy Frost is Director of Share Jesus International and Mission Director of Crossing London. He tweets @andythefrosty

JESUS' PRESENCE

I used to visit a husband and wife in a care home. Neither of them were Christians. He was a scientist and had a very high intellect. He used to work everything out in his mind and thought science was the answer to everything. One day when he was in terrible pain, I asked if I could pray with him and Jesus did the most amazing thing for him by taking away all his pain. This dear man, who was an atheist, experienced the presence of Jesus in his room. Both he and his wife came to faith at that time, which was just astonishing. It was completely God's work.

Buddy Reeve, founder of PARCHE, a local church project started in Eastbourne.

LEARN TO LISTEN

Joanne Cox challenges the catchphrase 'It's good to talk!'

As I was growing up, there was an advertising slogan spread far and wide through a series of clever adverts about a family trying to work out how to stay in touch. The slogan for the campaign was 'it's good to talk.' But what if the advertisers got it wrong?

What if the talking part is the wrong place to start? What if we stopped talking and started to listen? What might we discover?

As I sit and write this, I am in a coffee shop with conversations bubbling all around me, and my name written on the cup. Such is the desire for relationship and community today - we now have our names written on a throw-away cup, and are personally addressed as our drink is passed quasi-sacramentally across the service altar of coffee beans and caramel sauce.

Perhaps if I stop talking, I would start to glimpse a window into the souls and lives of the people around me: The exam worries. The business deal. The lecture notes. The relationship on the rocks. The child-carer at the end of their tether. The ambition. The fears. The loves and the losses.

What if sharing Jesus is not really about talking at all - but about listening. What if it is not about having the right answers in the conversation - the bait and switch response that leads the conversation onto one about faith or Jesus - but that we trust that God is in our midst? What if our job is to listen attentively; to listen to the Spirit, and to the other, and to our own thoughts and emotions?

What if all we have to do is to respond with a good question rather than the right answer?

Let's engage in some more holy eavesdropping. Let's hear the conversations around us for what they reveal - and for where the Holy Spirit is already at work. Let's learn some good questions that bring out the best in the person or people we are with.

Let's learn from the monastics who retreated from the world in order to pray and to study in order that they may be equipped to work and be hospitable and receive hospitality; in order that they might be better able to converse with others of faith and of none; in order that they were then able to retreat and study and pray about the people they met and the God they discovered.

It might be good to talk. But let us speak words of grace seasoned with salt. Let us dare to ask more questions because we are genuinely interested in the answer we might hear, and let us enable our conversation partners to take centre stage and to do much of the talking. Let's notice the potential of the kingdom of God through holy eavesdropping. Let's find good questions rather than right answers, and let's trust that God is up to something.

As Bono once apocryphally translated Psalm 46:10: 'Be still and know that I am God'... as 'Shut up, listen, and let me love you'.

Let's have more of those conversations.

Top tips:

- Write down five questions that bring out the best in another (What has inspired you this week? I'm in need of a book/film/music recommendation - what do you suggest? What's the most significant thing that is happening in your life at the moment?)

- Sit in a coffee shop or public space and engage in some holy eavesdropping. What themes do you hear about? What surprises or shocks you?

- Set an alarm for 10 minutes, and sit in silence. What do you hear? Where is God?

- Think about what makes a good conversation. Why was Jesus so good at conversations? What challenges you about these reflections?

Revd Dr Joanne Cox is the Learning and Development Co-ordinator for the London region of the Methodist Church. She is passionate about enabling people to communicate authentically and honestly, using contemporary media and ancient storytelling.

LISTEN & PRAY

You are not learning while you're talking. So learn to be quiet, observe what's going on, and listen for what God may want to say. When you don't know, don't speak. People respect you when you have the wisdom and humility to say, 'I'm not sure.'

If you conduct a post-mortem on your biggest failures, somewhere in the wreckage you'll find that you've forsaken the place of prayer.

Revd Yemi Adedeji, Associate Director of HOPE, is a pastor at Jesus House, London. He is also Director of the One People Commission for the Evangelical Alliance UK and is ordained as an Anglican Priest.

APPEAL TO REASON

Peter Saunders sets out 20 of the main arguments that have convinced Christians to embrace Christianity and give their lives to the service of Jesus Christ

In the interests of (relative) brevity I have stopped at 20 but I could have gone on and on….

1. The uniqueness of Jesus Christ

The life, teaching, extraordinary claims and miracles of Jesus Christ as recorded by eyewitnesses are best explained by him being God incarnate: the creator and sustainer of the universe who took on human flesh.

2. Jesus' death and resurrection

All historical records are agreed on the facts that Jesus was killed, that his dead body disappeared, that the disciples claimed to have seen him alive and that the church grew rapidly in the belief that he had been resurrected. His actual bodily resurrection in space-time history remains the best explanation for these observations.

3. The manuscript evidence for the New Testament

The life, death and resurrection of Jesus Christ are by far the best attested events in all antiquity in terms of the number of manuscripts recording them and the closeness in time of those hand-written records to the events they describe.

4. The uniqueness of the Bible

The uniqueness of the Bible in its continuity, circulation, translation, survival, teachings and influence along with its internal consistency despite consisting of 66 books written by over 40 authors on three continents over 1,500 years defies simple explanation and is fully consistent with its claim to be divine revelation.

5. Old Testament prophecy fulfilled in Christ

The 39 books that make up the Old Testament contain several hundred references to the coming Messiah concerning his life, death and resurrection which were written hundreds of years before Jesus' birth but were fulfilled during his life and confirm his credentials as the promised Messiah.

6. Biblical prophecy fulfilled in history

The hundreds of predictive prophecies in the Old Testament and New Testament about the fate of nations, empires and cities are consistent with supernatural revelation from a God outside the space-time continuum (Tyre, Sidon, Samaria, Gaza, Moab, Ammon, Edom, Egypt, Assyria, Babylon, Greece, Rome, Israel).

7. The uniqueness of the Christian experience

The shared testimony of a personal relationship with Jesus Christ by millions of people from diverse cultures, nations, personalities, professions and time periods is unparalleled by any other ideology and consistent with the existence of a God with a universal attraction to all kinds of human beings. Each testifies to finding peace, forgiveness, the power to change and new meaning, hope and purpose through Christ's death and resurrection.

8. The origin of the universe

Everything that began to exist has a cause and it is now virtually undisputed that the universe had a beginning. Any cause would have to be outside the material universe so would be timeless, spaceless, immaterial, personal and all-powerful – characteristics shared by the God of the Bible.

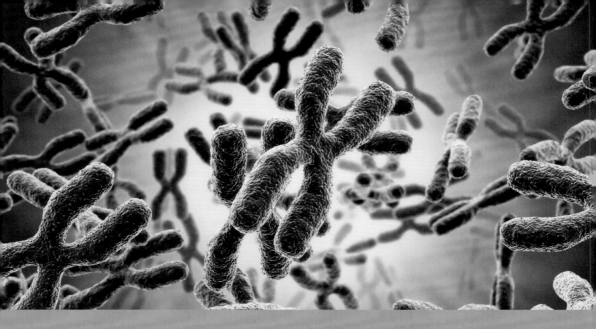

9. The fine tuning of the universe

In order for the universe to come into being and allow intelligent life to exist, it required an astonishing series of 'coincidences' to have occurred. The probability that the six dimensionless constants (N, Epsilon, Omega, Lambda, Q & D) would be tuned in such a way as to allow this purely by chance is infinitesimally small.

10. Biological complexity

Whilst it is widely recognised that random gene mutation, genetic drift and natural selection can account for a degree of biological descent with modification (evolution) the mechanisms by which proteins, DNA, unicellular organisms and new body plans could have arisen remain unexplained. Blind chance and necessity acting alone are not sufficient to account for the biological complexity that we observe on planet earth.

11. The rationality of the universe

The universe operates according to physical laws which are not merely regularities in nature but also mathematically precise, universal, 'tied together' and rationally intelligible.

These phenomena point to the existence of what Einstein called 'superior mind', 'illimitable superior spirit', 'superior reasoning force' and 'mysterious force that moves the constellations' and are fully consistent with the teachings of Christian theism.

12. The human mind

Human experience of free will, consciousness, self-awareness, conscience and a sense of meaning, purpose and destiny are all very difficult to explain within a purely materialist world view (ie the belief that nothing exists apart from matter, chance and time). These phenomena point to, and are consistent with, a reality existing beyond the material world and are consistent with the biblical teaching that human beings are made in the image of God.

13. The explanatory power of the Christian world view

The Christian theistic world view described by the parameters of creation, fall, redemption and consummation has considerable explanatory power in accounting for the existence of human complexity, creativity, love, suffering, disease, evil and hope.

14. The universality of spiritual belief and experience

The universal belief in, and experience of, a spiritual reality beyond the material world and in the existence of other intelligent beings in addition to human beings (gods, spirits, angels, demons, ghosts etc), along with the proliferation of different religions, is consistent with the Christian world view including the existence of a Devil whose intention is to deceive people into believing anything but the truth.

15. The moral law

The universality of moral beliefs and conscience, and the similarities of moral codes across times, continents and cultures, point to the existence of moral laws and a supernatural law giver. The moral laws outlined in the Decalogue (Ten Commandments) encapsulate these principles of respect for life, marriage, property and truth and their observance leads to more stable and enduring societies. These observations are consistent with the existence of a moral God who has designed human society to operate according to moral norms and who reveals moral principles.

16. Lives changed by Christian faith

The power of Christian faith and prayer to change behaviour and improve human functioning in restoring the lives of those suffering from addictions to drugs, alcohol, pornography and other enslaving activities or in reforming antisocial and criminal behaviour and strengthening marriages, families and societies is unparalleled.

17. Christian reformation of society

The reformation of British society in the 19th century (and many similar phenomena elsewhere in the world throughout history) through such moves as the abolition of slavery, child labour, child prostitution, prison reform and the establishment of schools and hospitals through the work of Wilberforce, Booth, Fry, the Clapham Sect and others was largely the result of the evangelical revival of the 18th century and lends strong support to the existence of a redemptive supernatural God who changes and shapes human lives and societies.

18. The work of Christian missions

The development of education, healthcare and societal reform in the developing world owes a great deal to the work of Christian missionaries motivated by the love of Christ who underwent great hardship and made great sacrifices to assist and empower those marginalised through ignorance, superstition or poverty. If Christianity were true we would expect it also to result in demonstrable good across nations and cultures.

19. The plausibility of Christian eschatology

The emergence of a one-world government under the leadership of an antichrist, antagonistic to God, based on the worship and pursuit of material things, strongly opposing Christian faith, dominating through economic control and resulting in massive environmental destruction seems increasingly plausible given recent historical experience and the current trajectory of world history.

20. The phenomenon of Israel

The history, laws, influence and endurance of the nation of Israel through over 4,000 years of world history whilst world empires have come and gone, the maintenance of its national identity and central place in world affairs through war, persecution and holocaust, its recent restoration to Palestine and the educational and cultural achievements of its people are unparalleled but fully consistent with its special status as described in the biblical record and teaching of Jesus Christ.

Dr Peter Saunders, formerly a General Surgeon, is CEO of the Christian Medical Fellowship. Read his blog at www.pjsaunders.blogspot.co.uk

TALK ABOUT WHAT YOU'VE SEEN, READ AND HEARD

Choose the right book, for the right time, for your friend, says Catherine Butcher

Art, music, films, plays, novels, biographies… what do the not-yet Christians you mix with enjoy and talk about?

Once, at the Edinburgh Festival, I saw a huge crowd gathered around two men arguing loudly with each other about who goes to heaven from the classic Calvinist and Arminian perspectives. It got people in the crowd talking: Can I choose heaven? Has God chosen me? How do I get to heaven? I wouldn't recommend rehearsing Christian doctrinal arguments as a way to share faith, but in the context of the Festival Fringe it provoked questions.

Talking to a friend or colleague about a book they are reading, a film you've watched together, or music they are listening to, is much more natural. I emphasise the books and music they are reading and listening to: start with your friend's interests. There are eternal themes running through many great works of literature, music and the arts.

Explore the archive of hundreds of articles and discussion guides reflecting on films, books, music, television and more in the CultureWatch Resources from Damaris (www.damaris.org). Whether you are reading a Dan Brown novel or Barack Obama's autobiography, there are themes and ideas which can spark a deeper conversation about faith.

And if you are reading the books your friends are reading, they might be interested in reading a Christian book you recommend. Here's a dozen I've recommended to friends. What would you recommend to your friends?

Don't forget to read it first and choose the right book, for the right time, for your friend.

- *Mud, Sweat and Tears* by Bear Grylls (Channel 4)
- *Chosen - An Autobiography* by Michele Guinness (Monarch)
- *Cherished* by Rachel Gardner (IVP)
- *The Hiding Place* by Corrie Ten Boom (Hodder & Stoughton)
- *Chronicles of Narnia* seven volumes by CS Lewis (Harper Collins)
- *God's Undertaker (Has Science buried God?)* John C Lennox (Lion)
- *The Reason for God: Belief in an Age of Scepticism* by Timothy Keller (Hodder & Stoughton)
- *If God Then What* by Andrew Wilson (IVP)
- *The Testament* by John Grisham (Arrow)
- *Redeeming Love* by Francine Rivers (Monarch)
- *Porridge and Passion: An Autobiography* by Jonathan Aitken (Continuum)
- *The Shack* by Wm Paul Young (Hodder Windblown)

WHO? - THE STORY OF JESUS

The life and death of Jesus were written from different viewpoints by Matthew, Mark and Luke and yet, they set out their material in a similar way. In *Who? – The Story of Jesus*, published by Bible Society, their words are blended together into a single faithful account, so the story of Jesus is brought to life through the eyes of his closest companions. Friends, sceptics and enemies all asked, 'Who is he?' Give someone the gift of *Who? – The Story of Jesus* and help them find out for themselves. Find out more at www.hopetogether.org.uk

Catherine Butcher is HOPE's Director of Communications, author of several books and editor of Day by Day with God *(BRF)*

MAKING CONNECTIONS

Beth Tash — looking for God at work in the clubbing culture

We need to have a language for our own story if we are to be able to share it. This doesn't mean that the gospel is different for each of us — just that we need to have a way of saying it that is true to the journey God has led us on. Authenticity is so important - if someone has asked you about your faith - they want to know your story - not someone else's!

I'm always on the look-out for connections between a person's story, my story and God's invitation to them. Those connections might be through things in the media, contemporary culture or common experience.

When I'm out clubbing I ask questions like: 'What is it you love about clubbing?' 'Have you ever had a God-experience?' 'Have you met a Christian before…?'

The main thing that God is teaching me, is that he draws people by his love — and most people love being loved! When we start by standing in God's shoes, and are filled with his love for ourselves and others; that's when the best conversations happen and we see glimpses of God's transforming love, truth and power in people and places — even in our nightclubs!

Beth Tash is a Pioneering Minister to the Night Time Economy in Leeds, where she is part of the clubbing scene and spends time talking to night-time workers, building links with local churches, praying with others and bringing 'a message of life and a mission of love'.

CREATION'S WOW FACTOR!

Our hearts long for heaven's beauty, says Catherine Butcher

Many people feel 'spiritual' when they are enjoying the natural world. Magnificent sunsets, majestic waves, beautiful flowers and delicate butterflies — they all have a 'wow' factor.

'The heavens declare the glory of God' says the Psalmist (Psalm 18:1) and Paul agrees: 'Since the creation of the world God's invisible qualities — his eternal power and divine nature — have been clearly seen … people are without excuse' (Romans 1:20).

Our hearts long for heaven's beauty (Ecclesiastes 3:11). But before people know God for themselves, they need those longings interpreted. As CS Lewis said: 'If we find ourselves with a desire that nothing in this world can satisfy, the most probable explanation is that we were made for another world.'

When fellow dog-walkers stop and stare at natural beauty, I often ask a question to point them from creation to the creator. What question would you ask?

Catherine Butcher, HOPE's Communications Director, studied Christian Spirituality (MA) at Heythrop College in London.

PLATFORM 9 ¾

Ask good questions, says Jason Gardner

What do the *Lord of the Rings, Harry Potter* and *Star Wars* films have in common? They all start with a young orphan boy who is living with his uncle. Frodo, Harry and Luke are alone in the universe and they're all in need of guidance. They get it in the form of a mystical elderly sage figure with white beard: Gandalf, Dumbledore, Obi Wan. Ask most people what God looks like and they'll say a Father Time figure, old, with a white beard. Interesting that! The most popular films of all time point to people who are orphaned in the universe but find a 'god' figure to guide them. Is the 'god-shaped hole' alive and well in our culture? Then add to that all the films that feature resurrection or messiah figures from Neo in *The Matrix* to E.T. the extra-terrestrial - a little green fellah with healing abilities.

Asking questions that take people deeper is about recognising the patterns. As Christian philosopher Paul Tillich points out, our culture advertises our hopes and fears. Take a look at some of our most enduring stories and they'll tell you what we live for and what we're afraid of. Why are Sunday nights on TV dominated by period dramas from Dickens' adaptations to *Downton Abbey*? Are we yearning for simpler times when choices around morals and relationships were clear cut, or do we just like the idea of wearing long dresses? And sci-fi films depict our fears clearly: the planet laid to waste by a comet or robots, or a virus caused by genetic modification gone wrong!

Then there are the 'have you noticed?' questions. Have you noticed how sporting events always bring people together? Have you noticed that there's a lot of love for the royal family right now? Have you noticed how anxiety levels in Britain seem to be on the rise?

Good conversations begin with good questions. And good questions begin with listening to and observing the culture around us.

Jason Gardner is youth pastor at St Peter's Harrow and a speaker and writer on intergenerational issues

DOES MY LIFE COUNT?

The world around us is suffering, says Josh Jost. Do we have answers?

People in our communities are losing sleep, worrying about relationships, money, career, the future... and more. Do they know that we have answers for them?

It's easy to think that suffering only exists in poverty-stricken parts of the world, but many people around us are in silent agony: 1 in 4 people in the UK suffers from a mental illness, the vast majority of them with depression and anxiety. According to the World Health Organisation, mental illness has a more detrimental effect on wellbeing than physical disease.

Over many discussions with non-Christian friends, as well as research on current social trends, I've come to the conclusion that what people are most lacking is 'significance', which is one of the reasons that we are so obsessed with celebrity culture.

Why do we crave significance?

In our scientifically-minded western world we have become entrenched in a philosophy called reductionism which, in simple terms, states that life has no greater significance. And if life has no significance then, logically, neither do you or I.

This mindset reduces our purpose down to mere survivalism and has filled the planet with all manner of greed, warmongering, abuse and corruption as people fight for their own survival.

The reason we crave significance is because we feel fearful and powerless in a world that is falling apart. This powerlessness bleeds into causing us to feel like nothing we do matters. So instead we become depressed or turn to hedonism, escapism, career changes, materialism or new relationships.

According to leading game designer Jane McGonigal, people are leaving the real world en masse for the virtual reality of the online gaming world because, in that world, they can be 'super-empowered hopeful individuals'.

So what is our answer to this?

When I speak to non-Christians, I explain to them why significance is the biggest need today and how Jesus came to build a new world (kingdom) not based on personal survival but on selfless life-giving, and that God invites all of us to discover our eternal significance and destiny by becoming his sons and daughters and joining him in his mission to bring the wonder of heaven to earth.

You may think that people are put off by the idea of self-sacrifice but you would be surprised how many are longing for something to give their lives to.

Joshua Jost, a Christian author, has developed the World Within programme to support churches in 21st century evangelism. www.WorldWithin.org

ENJOY LIFE!

'You make known to me the path of life; you will fill me with joy in your presence, with eternal pleasures at your right hand' Psalm 16:11

Do our lives show what 'abundant life' looks like? asks Ann Holt

One of the caricatures that today's Christians have to live down is that of the Victorian killjoy. Ellen Glasgow described her Presbyterian father 'as entirely unselfish, and in his long life he never committed a pleasure!' Unfortunately, it's not very different today! Often, as a result of the public debates over moral boundaries, Christians are thought of as disapproving rather than as people with the full or abundant lives that Jesus says he came to give us (John 10:10).

One of the fruits of the Spirit is joy! (Galatians 5:22-23). Joy is a product of abundance. Knowing that God desires our pleasure should give us the kind of joy that underpins us even in the times of testing and trouble which none of us escapes. The pursuit and measurement of happiness are current hot topics because true happiness seems so elusive to so many. The world is searching! Does our different quality of life in Christ make them even curious?

We live in an age whose psychology is characterised by hedonism which is often mistaken for pleasure. The enormous entertainment industry is a sign of a bored society. In the words of the late Neil Postman we are being 'entertained to death'. When we debate moral issues, such as pornography which is now such a huge part of the entertainment industry, we should do so in a way that positively demonstrates the virtues of boundaries and moderation, and their contribution to individual and common good.

Realistically, sins do masquerade as pleasures. At the heart of our fallen world is a delusion that true pleasure comes from asserting human autonomy and going our own way, rather than seeking the perfect will of God. We need to be able to challenge the wisdom of this by our well-lived lives as well as our public arguments.

Psalm 126 rejoices that: 'When the Lord restored the fortunes of Zion we were like those who dream. Then our mouth was filled with laughter and our tongue with shouts of joy.'

Do our dreams fill us with laughter and joy?

Nobel Prize-winning psychologist and economist, Daniel Kahneman, has discovered that much of our pleasure comes from anticipation and good memories. Remembering what God has done for us and living in the anticipation of a new heaven and earth is the basis of an everlasting pleasure; looking forward to the next holiday is just a pale shadow. Sharing our excitement about both in our conversations is a place to start dispelling that killjoy image with our friends!

Canon Dr Ann Holt OBE works for Bible Society.

WHAT WOMEN WANT

Build trust and show real acceptance, says Emma Ingram

Although we should be cautious of generalisations, especially on gender issues, at the heart of every woman is a longing to be needed and appreciated. To connect and take conversations to the next level, we need to show that we value the women we mix with and we want to listen to what they have to say.

Two key things you can offer are time and a listening ear. Some women fear being judged by Christians; that's a real barrier to coming to church, so build trust and show real acceptance of women as they are. Jesus spent time with people, listening and caring. Think of ways to bless the women that you know, whether it is offering to help her look after her kids or an elderly dependent relative, or asking her for a coffee. Gestures of love can speak volumes and deepen friendship.

In all situations, the key is staying in tune with God. It's worth remembering that God wants that person to know him more than you do, and he wants to use us to speak to them through him.

Emma Ingram is part of New Life Church, Croydon and is a freelance graphic designer.

HAVE FUN TOGETHER

Build friendships with the women you meet at work, in the gym or in your neighbourhood. As extended family networks break down, the church has a key part to play in building strong communities and reaching out to people who are isolated. Conversations flow more easily when you've spent time together having fun.

Here are some ideas to try:

- Hold a chick-flick night – don't forget the popcorn.
- Sing-a-long with *The Sound of Music* or *Sunshine on Leith* – invite everyone to come dressed in costume, give out the words to the songs, and turn up the volume on the DVD-player for a riotous night in!
- Join your local fundraising marathon to raise money for breast cancer charities.
- Bake a cake every month to give away to one of your Facebook friends.
- Hold a Pamper Party.
- In Fairtrade Fortnight, hold a fairtrade event with fairtrade teas, coffees and goodies to eat, plus fairtrade products to buy.
- Make Christmas cards together.
- Take turns with your friends to hold meals with food from different countries – this works particularly well if your area includes people with lots of different ethnic roots.
- If you've got young children at home, get together with other mums in the school holidays to take children to the park for a treasure hunt, game of football or a picnic.
- Looking after an elderly relative? Form a Facebook group to keep in touch online – and if relatives are able to get out and about, pool resources with other carers to book a wheelchair-friendly, mini-bus for an outing.

MAKE SOME MATES

Carl Beech makes the case for reaching men

A Tearfund survey in 2007 found that 75% of British men were antagonistic or apathetic towards the gospel. In 2003 *Evangelicals Now* found that if you introduce a child to Jesus, 3.5% of the time the rest of the family would find Jesus; if you introduce a mother to Jesus then 17% of the time, the rest of the family would follow. The statistic for men was that 93% of the time, if you introduce a father to Jesus, the rest of the family would follow. That makes a serious case for investing more into reaching and keeping men. Even if these statistics are 50% wrong (a huge margin of error) then that's still persuasive!

CVM (Christian Vision for Men) advise what we call a '4 level' approach to reaching men. In a nutshell the strategy is this:

Level 1

Do something fun that helps build relationships. Men communicate 'over the shoulder' in the context of activity. You don't need a talk; just the conduct of your lives will do at this stage. Do stuff that's laugh-out-loud funny, maybe involves food and gives a chance for relationships to develop. There is an epidemic of loneliness and a real lack of joy amongst men. Get out there and make some mates. Get together as a band of brothers. Create some memories and moments and the men will start to open up.

Level 2

This is any event with a speaker. Make it a generous and well-hosted night or morning and get a speaker who has an interesting story about their life and faith. Ideally the talk should be about 20-25 minutes and leave time for conversation. For many churches, this is the start and end point of men's work. We suggest it is the middle stage and really only works effectively if the other elements are happening as well.

Level 3

This is a course such as Alpha. We find that a course just for men really works well, partly because men are often reluctant to speak about what's on their minds with women present. (Some issues on men's minds, which are barriers to faith, can be quite sensitive!)

Level 4

Easier said than done, level four is the man-friendly church! This is quite an involved subject that we don't have space for here. Suffice to say, we need to look at teaching styles, worship culture and the life of the church in the week. We also need to consider the look and feel of the church as well.

Carl Beech leads an international evangelistic men's movement called Christian Vision for Men (CVM). @carlfbeech CVM has produced a DVD called Men *which unpacks this issue in much more detail and is available from www.cvm.org.uk*

Six Men Encountering God by Brad Lincoln (BRF) – stories of six very different men finding faith – a great book to give away.

USING SOCIAL MEDIA

Engage with a diverse, world-wide audience, says Darren Quinnell

The way in which society communicates is changing. The 21st century has brought with it the Social Revolution, what some people are calling the biggest culture jump since the Industrial Revolution. If this is the case then Christians need to use this new social media just like Christians used Johannes Gutenberg's printing press to publish the first printed Bibles.

Christians are still learning how to best use social media. Some are very sceptical, saying it is creating loneliness and taking away privacy; others question the value of relationships made online.

But Christians have always communicated through the media available to them at the time, and social media is no different. Social media offers Christians powerful ways to engage with a diverse audience and morally-challenging world. The key is learning how best to communicate opinions and faith with respect and integrity.

Starting God conversations

Here are some tips to help you start conversations about God using social media and to provide a natural and positive process for your social media feeds:

- Be an example through your actions, language and attitude.
- Respect the opinions of others.
- Emotions don't come across in text, so be careful how your words could be read.
- Manage your conversations; remember that you are in control of your social networks.
- Don't aim to start conversations that simply cause a heated reaction.
- Don't worry about stats and followers; quality over quantity is what really matters.
- Christian lingo can alienate people; make sure statuses are clear of it.
- God doesn't need a separate status, involve him in your everyday statuses in subtle ways.
- See what's first being said and engage with it, rather than starting a new conversation.
- Make sure you respond to comments; make sure people feel they have been heard.
- With access to a global stage, highlight campaigns that promote godly justice.
- Offer prayer for people, by asking them to send prayer requests to your inbox.
- Scroll through your wall and feeds to pray for individuals that appear.

Darren Quinnell is the Director of Message to the Masses, which aims to help young people understand their faith while also resourcing them to defend that faith through online multimedia and social networks.
www.messagetothemasses.com

WORDS & ACTIONS ONLINE

Words and actions online can help you share faith, says Steven Harper

Just as you would in 'real life' there are two key ways that you can share faith online: actions and words. You don't need to post Christian stuff all the time to show you are a Christian!

Words

What we post, and how we post, (as Darren says on the page opposite) can be really important. It could be the first reflection of Christianity that someone sees and interacts with.

Our language needs to be relevant: anything you post should be readable and understandable to anyone (especially someone with no knowledge of God). Jesus used simple words, simple stories and love to relate to people. Use words that make Christian faith accessible to ordinary people.

Actions

How is it possible to show love through actions online? Start with the small things... Take an interest in your friends' posts (both Christian and non-Christian). Interact with them. Likes on Facebook, and Favourites on Twitter are great ways of showing your appreciation of something without having to use words.

No matter who we are, we all love encouragement, and that is where actions online can really help. Use your online spaces to encourage non-Christians. Follow and support organisations that do good works, whether they are Christian or not. What you like and who you follow are important parts to the process of sharing your faith, because without using direct words you are showing people what you care about, and what you believe in.

Be relational. Being online gives you a great insight into the world. You can easily find out what people are talking about. Get involved with discussions. Find the conversations and people that relate to your life, loves and faith, and get involved, build relationships, and start sharing your faith!

Steven Harper is the Community Manager for YesHEis in the UK.

WEBSITES AND ONLINE RESOURCES

Here are two websites to help you share faith online

www.yesheis.com
www.messagetothemasses.com

Here's a source of interesting and thought-provoking social media content

www.upworthy.com

Here are some websites to help not-yet Christians to find out more about faith in Jesus

www.christianity.org.uk
www.lookingforgod.com
www.trypraying.co.uk
www.iamsecond.com
www.rejesus.co.uk
www.uncover.org.uk

ACT KINDLY

Catch the kindness bug, says Andy Hawthorne

Often our schools teams here at the Message Trust in Manchester will ask 'what's the first word you think of when you hear the word Christian?' Top of the charts is 'boring' followed by 'weird' and 'religious', how sad is that? We really do have an image problem in the church. One that I believe will only be changed if we stop being boring, religious and weird and start simply being kind.

How amazing would it be if the church of Jesus was known for being the kind of people who are not just kind because it is 'the Noise weekend' or a HOPE 2014 event but because day in day out they are following Jesus who personified kindness 24/7 and have well and truly got the kindness bug.

Clearly the greatest kindness we can offer anyone is to share with them a message that can completely change their eternal destiny and give them something to live for today and always. It should always be our desire to share that message with as many people as possible, but it's also pretty obvious that nothing softens people's hearts to Jesus like a healthy dose of kindness.

Don't you love the fact that Jesus' nickname was 'Friend of Sinners'? And wouldn't it be amazing if more of us asked two questions on the back of that? Firstly where are the people who haven't had their sins forgiven by Jesus in my neighbourhood? And secondly, what can I do to befriend them, not in a weird 'you are my latest target' kind of way but because the love of God is in our lives and we absolutely cannot keep it in.

Andy Hawthorne OBE is an evangelist, author and leader of the Message Trust, a Christian mission organisation based in Manchester, England.

BLESS AND SERVE YOUR COMMUNITY

Could you take on the responsibility to pray for and serve the people in the street where you live, work or pass through regularly? Be on the look-out for opportunities to serve your neighbours.

Link with others sharing a similar vision through:

- Love Your Street
  www.loveyourstreet.org.uk

- Neighbourhood Prayer Network
  www.neighbourhoodprayer.net

These networks aim to see every street in the UK covered in Christian prayer.

CONVERSATION-STARTERS

Paul Griffiths introduces two tools to prompt questions and help build relationships

Wouldn't it be great to have meaningful conversations with our family, friends and acquaintances about the issues that really matter in life? Some of us are better at this than others - here are two resources to help you get started.

Table Talk is a series of games designed to help people engage in meaningful conversations. There are games that are themed: Table Talk for friends; blokes; university students; Messy Church; Easter; youth packs for four different age-groups and a family pack for Christmas. Each game has six big questions.

How is it used? Ruth Rice, a church leader in Nottingham, says 'Table Talk has reshaped how we do evangelism.

'We began running a Table Talk group at a local café in the suburb of Nottingham. We book the same table each week and everyone arrives from about 7.30pm grabbing a drink and joining in the discussion. Anyone can start by picking up a card from the Table Talk selection. It's great and really natural.

'We have a regular Table Talk group now on Tuesday nights of between six and 12 people, many in their 20s and 30s ... a mixture of atheists, agnostics, Christians, and others on a journey from belonging to believing.

'Our regular atheist, who would now call himself an agnostic, has begun reading his Bible from cover to cover and is writing his own questions. Three people have realised they have changed sides somewhere in the process of discussions, like crossing a mountain border on a long hike yet not being quite sure where the border was.'

To find out more visit www.table-talk.org

PUZZLING QUESTIONS

The six-week Puzzling Questions course explores the most popular questions asked by those who are outside the church but interested in finding out more.

With a format of food, presentation, then discussion, the centre-piece of the course are the six 30-minute, magazine-style DVD programmes which are used to present the material. These include Vox Pop comments from people filmed on the street, poetry reading by Stewart Henderson, a two-minute personal story of what that question means to an individual, and the big interview - a Michael Parkinson-type interview on the question under discussion.

Find out more at www.puzzlingquestions.org.uk

Paul Griffiths is a member of the Archbishop of Canterbury's College of Evangelists. He leads the Ugly Duckling Company and his son describes him as the Homer Simpson of spiritual insight.

WINSOME

Pray and expect to have conversations about faith with the people you meet, says Hugo Anson

We all have friends, relatives, colleagues, acquaintances and people in our communities who we would love to see become Christians. Use the five simple WinSome steps outlined below and pray that God will help you to build his kingdom.

The WinSome initiative helps us all to focus on this personal ministry and starts with each of us praying for our family members and friends who we wish to introduce to Christ.

Please encourage your congregation to commit to this vital evangelistic outreach.

Look around

God wants everyone to know him and to respond to the love of his Son, Jesus Christ. So first, we ask people to look around. Are there family, friends, colleagues, acquaintances and people who you would like to see come to Christ? Write down the names, in faith, expecting to have an opportunity to talk to them about the hope Jesus gives.

Look up

The next step is to pray every day for these people. Praying that hearts and minds will be open to God's love and faithfulness, forgiveness and compassion. Pray too for God's wisdom as you witness.

Look out

It's important you share your faith in natural ways which show Christ's love in action. We encourage people to build real and meaningful relationships with those for whom they are praying, and to be prepared to answer spiritual questions as hearts begin to open to God.

Look forward

If the people you are praying for are not used to going to church or attending Christian events, it's much easier if you go with them. We encourage people to invite their friends to church, and to events when they can find out more about Jesus.

Look after

Some friends, family, acquaintances and colleagues will accept Jesus. Praise God! The next stage is to help them grow in their faith. Stay close and help these new Christians as they step out on their faith journey. If there is not an immediate response, continue to be a friend, and continue to pray for them.

Who to add to your WinSome list

Start with two or three people you are already praying for, then add more people to your list. For example, add:

- Someone who is being prayed for by your housegroup/church.
- A neighbour from your street who starts talking to you during the week after you start prayer walking.
- A mum you meet at the school gate who says, 'I don't know what the world's coming to?'
- Someone you meet during an outreach or social action project.

Pray by yourself, in your home group and in your church meetings. Meet with friends to pray together. Prayer-walk around your area,

FAITH FLAGS

A Medical Student's Tale: 'I have the habit of wearing something that might be a talking point for people. On this occasion I had a small fish badge. It was a Friday evening and an old lady on the ward asked me "What does that fish mean?"

'"It means I have faith in Jesus and the living God."

'She wanted to talk about it and we had a brief chat, but I said I needed to hurry to catch the last train home and we could continue on Monday if she wanted. She said she'd like that and I rushed off.

'On Monday morning I couldn't find her on the ward... she'd died over the weekend. I have always felt a bit stupid about it – what did a train matter if she wanted me to stay and chat? I remember her and try to make the most of every opportunity.'

Former General Surgeon and inner city GP, Graham McAll: 'Visual faith flags are commonly used... I have used various pictures in my consulting room. One is of a shaft of sunlight catching a beautiful flower of paradise, a Strelitzia, against a black background. This has often brought comment and questions from my patients. I tell them it reminds me of my patients and their illnesses – the hope of something remarkable happening in a dark place, or words to that effect, or to remind me that Jesus is a specialist in bringing good out of evil times. My response to their question would depend on them and varies a lot.'

At a Given Moment - Faith Matters in Healthcare Encounters by Graham McAll (CMF)

host a prayer event or start a prayer 'boiler room'. Set up a regular WinSome prayer meeting for your area or local church and pray for individuals who are about to be, being or have become Christians.

Hugo Anson, along with his wife Sharon, leads the Grassroots Trust (www.grassroots.org.uk) - a Christian mission agency which specialises in developing innovative evangelism, social action and prayer projects in the UK and around the world. Hugo is serving Crossing London by thinking up ways to get Christians praying.

GOD MENDS BROKEN RELATIONSHIPS

"When Jesus himself presents the gospel … he has something profound and simple to say to everyone that he meets"

The gospel is like a beautiful multifaceted diamond in our hands. Not only do we hold and guard the most amazing treasure, there are also so many different aspects to appreciate. Because of this we should be particularly careful not to be restricted by simplistic outlines which run the risk of presenting an emaciated, soulless set of bullet points instead of the splendour of Jesus in all his fullness. When Jesus himself presents the gospel it never sounds formulaic like a recycled old joke or an overused cliché: he has something profound and simple to say to everyone that he meets, and surely this is what we aspire to as we join in with the work of the Holy Spirit and witness to Jesus.

To help me make sure that I convey something of the grand sweep of the Bible's story and don't downplay the scale of what Jesus' life, death and resurrection have accomplished, I often use the mental framework outlined below. I share this in the hope that it might help you to tell the gospel in fresh and inspiring ways, uniquely tailored to each person you have opportunity to talk to, not so that you would slavishly recite it and lose sight of the diamond in your hands.

Created

The opening chapters of the Bible describe life as God designed it, and from the outset his intentions for his world are characterised by love. In fact you can see four dimensions to the love that God intended for us. Firstly we were made to love and be loved by God — he wants a genuine personal relationship with us. Secondly we were made to love and be loved by others — note that the first thing that is described as wrong in the universe is loneliness and isolation (Genesis 2). Thirdly we were made to love and care for the world around us — God made our world full of opportunities for exploration, creativity, wonder and potential for us to make something of it. Fourthly because humanity would know love and security with God, with others and our environment humans are able to love and appreciate themselves.

Corrupted

When humankind believed the lie that God did not really love us or trust us (Genesis 3), we damaged our relationship not just with God but with everything and everyone. Just as ink spilled in a tank of water doesn't just affect one portion of the water but instead spreads throughout the whole tank contaminating all of it, so human rebellion against God has had a corrupting influence on everything in the world. Firstly we are alienated from God — our sin means that God as the just judge of the universe must punish human wickedness. Secondly we are alienated from others — we live in a world of broken human relationships, abuse, injustice, bullying, war and racism. Thirdly due to the disruption to the created order, even our world is not as it should be — from viruses to volcanoes from weeding to global warming. Fourthly now when many people look at themselves in a mirror they don't like what they see — eating disorders, mental health conditions, self-doubt, self-harm, low self-esteem are all symptomatic of that brokenness in our relationship with ourselves.

Amidst the brokenness of these relationships we can still see many glimpses of beauty. Sometimes we sense directly the presence of God or sometimes friends give us a taste of genuine sacrificial love. Often in nature we are hit by the sheer wonder of creation, and often we sense those things we were designed to enjoy all the time — satisfaction, contentment, security. So although no part of human existence is untouched by sin — no part is completely without the gracious benevolence of God either.

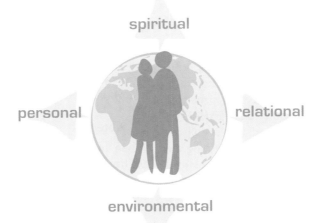

spiritual

personal

relational

environmental

Repaired

The coming of Jesus was signalled and prepared for in God's dealings with the world through the Jewish people over thousands of years. But in Jesus we see God become human, perfectly imaging the character of God that every other human being has failed to achieve. Jesus shows us human relationships being repaired and restored as he makes fellow disciples out of enemies, family out of outcasts, and Christians out of social misfits. In Jesus' life and miracles we glimpse nature being restored – as he feeds the hungry, heals the sick or stills the storm. When people encounter Jesus their perception of themselves changes too - lepers, fishermen, tax-collectors, thieves and adulterers are all personally transformed. It is supremely in the cross of Jesus that we see sin and God's anger at sin dealt with once and for all as Jesus offers himself as a sacrifice for sin and shows us what love truly looks like. At the cross we see exactly how valuable we are to God, and we witness the beginning of God making all things new.

Restored

The Bible promises that one day God will live perfectly on earth with his people (Revelation 21). One day all wars will cease and from all nations we will live together as one united family. One day there will be no more death, disease or disaster as God restores the heavens and the earth to good-as-new condition. God will wipe away every tear and we will see him and ourselves as we truly are. So Christians live in hope that all four of those broken relationships will be fully restored. In the meantime we are given the power of God's Spirit as a guarantee of that sure destiny, and to help us give people around us a taste of what is to come.

Dr Krish Kandiah is Executive Director of Churches in Mission at the Evangelical Alliance. He blogs on mission and evangelism at www.krishk.com and tweets at @krishk

GOD IS LOVE

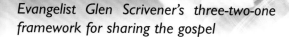

Evangelist Glen Scrivener's three-two-one framework for sharing the gospel

Three — God is three persons united in love. Before there was a world, there were Three. Who are they? Jesus kept talking about his Father (and his love) and the Spirit (and his joy). Before the world began, God was a family of love: Father, Son and Holy Spirit. And their love was too good to keep to themselves. They made a world so that billions more can share in the love of the Three.

Two — The world is shaped by two representatives. God placed one man, Adam, at the head of the world to bless it and care for it. Yet through mistrust, Adam turned from God and plunged the world down into death and hell. We all share in this broken humanity and feel the curse of this broken world.

But there is a second man, Jesus Christ. Jesus is the Son of God who became our brother at Christmas. He entered into our broken world, stepping into our shoes. He lived our life for us and on the cross he faced the death and hell that belong to us. Three days later he rose up to a new kind of human life — the head of a new kind of world.

So who do we belong to? Adam or Jesus?

One — The Bible says that, from birth, all humanity is one with Adam. We are united to the old, Adam-like way and naturally share in his life, death and judgement. But God doesn't want anyone to be separated from his love. Jesus stands, arms wide open, offering one-ness with himself. If we trust him we become united to Jesus like in a marriage. All that is ours (our sin and judgement) becomes his - he pays it all off on the cross. All that is his (his righteousness and future) becomes ours.

In union with Jesus we share now in his family — filled with his Spirit and adopted by his Father. And when he comes again we will also share in his immortal, physical future.

The *Three* invite you in.
The *Two* divide the world.
Who are you *One* with?

Watch 321 the animated video. Glen Scrivener talking through Three-Two-One on YouTube 'Glen Scrivener explains the Good News in 3 2 1' and visit www.three-two-one.org

Glen Scrivener is an evangelist who is part of a town centre Anglican church on the south coast of England.

WE CAN BE FRIENDS WITH GOD

Phil Knox explores the ultimate antidote to today's loneliness epidemic

We are more connected than ever before by technology, but the quality of our connections has diminished. More people live alone and one million British people have been classed as chronically lonely.

We are created for friendship - life is designed to be a team game rather than an individual pursuit. Right at the beginning of humanity's story, God recognises this and says, 'it is not good for the man to be alone,' and so creates a companion for him. But more importantly we were created for friendship with God. Throughout the pages of the Bible we see God's desire for friendship with us: from the way in which he invites Adam to name the animals with him (Genesis 2:19) to his face to face conversations with Moses (Exodus 33:11); from the tenderness of God's protection of the people of Israel (Isaiah 40) to Jesus' explicit expression of friendship with the disciples (John 15:15).

Friendship is a two-way process and friends can hurt and reject one another. The same is true

with our friendship with God. We are not born friends with God, we have to make friends and like a continuous Facebook friendship request, the offer is always open. Most of us know the feeling when a friendship breaks down. It can feel like there is a tangible barrier between you and the other person. When we do things wrong, however small or big our fault, this distances us from God's friendship and forms a barrier between him and us. The Bible uses words like 'separate', 'far away', 'foreigners' and 'aliens' (Ephesians 2). The big story running through the Bible is of God's efforts to restore his friendship with humanity.

In today's hyper-connected world we have many ways of communicating with one another through cyberspace. But nothing comes close to the tangible presence of a friend. So God's ultimate expression of friendship comes when he takes on flesh and blood, and spends time on earth with us. Jesus' life on earth embodies God's offer of friendship.

But not only that, Jesus' death and resurrection make the friendship possible. Without them, there would still be an ever-present chasm between us and God. Jesus acts as peacemaker, mediating between us and God. His actions on the cross and in the grave take on and defeat the barrier of the wrong that prevents a friendship with God. As Paul puts it in Ephesians 2:14: 'For he himself is our peace, who has made the two groups one and has destroyed the barrier, the dividing wall of hostility.'

Invitations need a response. An outstretched hand needs shaking, a Friend request needs accepting, a wedding card needs an RSVP. God's offer of friendship to us needs us to say yes.

At the heart of every friendship is trust. The best of friends trust one another with their lives. Accepting God's offer of friendship involves trusting him with our life. Friendship is also costly. Deep friendship is not as simple

as clicking 'accept' on Facebook. It involves giving ourselves, our time and energy. The cost of being friends with God is giving all of our lives to that friendship and trusting him with every decision.

The best friends are also regular and intimate communicators. Friendship with God involves constant listening and talking, time spent getting to know God through his story, the Bible, and regularly listening and speaking to him in prayer.

Consider for a moment the amazing invitation to be friends with the creator of the universe and invite others to do the same.

Phil Knox is the Director of Church Resources at Youth for Christ. www.yfc.co.uk

CONTAGIOUS CHRISTIANITY

I started attending a youth club in Stockport when I was 11. After a period of attending twice a week, not only did I see my youth leaders' commitment in giving up their time, but I saw their passion for Jesus. My youth leaders invested so much time into me and built relationships where we could chat, not only about God stuff but other stuff going on at home and school! For me they walked the talk in their relationship with Jesus.

I made a choice to follow Jesus when I was 13, after watching them and seeing if they actually believed what they said! Now, 21 years later, I am thankful to God for them as they nurtured me and encouraged me to get involved in church.

Jonny Gios is a community worker and a district youth officer for the Methodist Church.

GOOD NEWS FOR THE PLANET

Christians offer hope for people and for the planet, says Ruth Valerio

Climate change, overpopulation, species extinction, the coral reefs dissolving, pollution… is there any hope for this world? Increasingly it looks like the answer is no. In fact there is a dark pessimism overshadowing scientists and conservationists who work in this area.

But one interesting thing is emerging. A recent report from the Environment Agency brought together the views of 25 environmental experts (scientists, activists and policy makers) to produce a list of the '50 things that will save the planet'. To many people's surprise, second

only to reducing our energy usage, was the statement that 'religious leaders need to make the planet their priority'. And the Environment Agency is not alone: Lord May, former Chief Scientific Advisor to the government, said something similar a few years ago.

As Christians, we have something unique to offer: hope. The gospel is a hopeful message and it is exciting that we can be a part of it, sharing and bringing that hope to both people and planet.

So how can we do that? There are many different things we can look at, so this is by no means 'the definitive way,' but I would like to suggest that there are five key points that are helpful to explain to people when we share this gospel of hope with our words (and I'm sure I hardly need say that our words will only make sense if they are an explanation of our actions).

1. God made the world and he loves it

God is the creator of the world and he thinks it is, 'very good' (Genesis 1:31). God is involved with his creation, sustaining it and caring for it (Psalm 65:9-13; Matthew 10:29; Hebrews 1:3; Colossians 1:16-17). This is not anti-evolution (the Genesis creation stories teach us theology not science), but an affirmation that this world has a greater being behind it and has a purpose.

2. God created us to look after the world

We are created beings, part of the whole community of creation, one part of an intricately connected ecosystem. But we have also been given a special task: to look after the rest of what God has made (Genesis 1:26-28; 2:15). This is not an optional extra for a few keen environmentalists, but a fundamental part of what it means to be human. We become less than human when we lose that connection.

3. It has gone wrong because of us

It is a sad truth that the many problems our world and its inhabitants face are caused by human activity. Our wrongdoing does not only separate us from God and have human consequences - it also has ecological consequences (Hosea 4:1-3; Amos 8:1-8). We bear the guilt for the state our world is in (Isaiah 24: 4-6) and each one of us has a responsibility to act.

4. Jesus came to this earth for the whole world

The good news is that God is working to put back to rights what has gone wrong. This is why Jesus died, to restore to himself ALL things (Colossians 1:19-20). Jesus' life, death and resurrection were not only for the benefit of people but for the benefit of the whole created order (Romans 8: 19-22).

5. God has a purpose for the world and asks us to join in

God has promised that, when Jesus returns, this world will be radically renewed: all that is evil will be destroyed; all that is good will shine out (2 Peter 3:10; Revelation 21:1 – 22:6). The gospel invitation is to follow Jesus and join in: to play our part in working to see justice, peace and ecological healing.

So let's remember:

- God made this world and loves it
- God has created us to look after it
- The ecological problems we see in the world are our fault
- Jesus died not just for human beings but to put to rights the whole created order
- The invitation is for us to follow Jesus and play our part in his plans.

Dr Ruth Valerio is Theology Director for the Christian environmental charity, A Rocha UK. See www.arocha.org.uk and www.ruthvalerio.net. She is part of Revelation Church, Chichester.

SCIENCE AND FAITH

'For me, as a Christian believer, the beauty of the scientific laws reinforces my faith in an intelligent, divine creator. The more I understand science, the more I believe in God, because of my wonder at the breadth, sophistication, and integrity of his creation.'

John C. Lennox in *God and Stephen Hawking*. John Lennox is Professor of Mathematics at the University of Oxford and Fellow in Mathematics and the Philosophy of Science at Green Templeton College.

FOUR SYMBOLS

Simple symbols to give a framework for sharing God's good news

God loves me!

The four points are an overview of the entire Bible and the first thing you need to know is that God is crazy about you! His love is unlimited and completely unconditional. There is nothing you can do to make God love you any more or any less than he does right now. There is nothing God wants more than to love and be loved by you.

Bible: Psalm 100:5, 1 John 3:16

I've messed up

Sadly we have all been separated from God's love by something the Bible calls sin. Simply put, sin is choosing to live for ourselves rather than God. We sin when we ignore God, break his laws and do things our own way. Sin destroys relationships with friends, with family and with God. The Bible says sin ultimately brings death.

Bible: Isaiah 59:2, Romans 6:23

Jesus died for me

The third point is probably one of the most well-known facts in the history of mankind but is often misunderstood. The key is to realise that the penalty for sin is death. We've all sinned and we all deserve to die. But God, who is full of mercy, loved you so much that he sent Jesus to come and die in your place. Jesus died so that we can have eternal life.

Bible: 1 John 4:9-10, Romans 5:8

I need to decide

God has done everything he can to demonstrate just how important you are to him. It is now up to you to decide what you want to do. God is offering you life in all its fullness for all eternity. All you need to do is accept that you've sinned, ask God's forgiveness and decide to live the rest of your life only for him. The choice is yours.

Bible: Deuteronomy 30:19, 1 John 1:9

Find out more at www.living4god.net

FINDING FREEDOM

The gospel means an end to shame and condemnation. Ben Cooley explains

She was 19 years old when Hope for Justice rescued her. She had spent the previous five years being trafficked throughout Europe's sex industry. She was a British girl forced to work in brothels where men had three to five minutes of her time. She kept count of how many men she was forced to service each day. One day she wrote down the number 117.

Hope for Justice knew her as Sarah, the name she went by. It had taken months of investigation to identify her. Now investigators had orchestrated her safe collection and, after talking with her for a long time, she broke down: 'You can call me Emma*... no-one has called me Emma since this all began.'

Sometimes we forget what the good news of the gospel really is. As Paul says: 'There is now no condemnation for those who are in Christ Jesus, because through Christ Jesus the law of the Spirit who gives life has set you free from the law of sin and death' (Romans 8:1-2).

No condemnation. Freedom. No shame.

Freedom comes from knowing the truth (John 8:31-32). The world will not be free until it knows the truth, and so we must tell the truth about how God feels about us; the truth about our worth, and how beautifully we are made; the truth about how Christ died so that we need never experience shame or death.

Most victims of trafficking have been lied to: promised legitimate jobs, a future, opportunities; that if they work hard enough they'll be set free. Recovery can only start when they recognise the truth. In a similar way, we can set people free by being speakers of truth.

When you become a Christian, the gospel doesn't stop there; the baton isn't for you to cling to but to pass on. God has relentlessly pursued us with passion and compassion, so that the least and the lost aren't left in the dark without the Good News to light their way to freedom. It's our task to spread that Good News.

No one is going to hear about Jesus if we don't tell them. But no one will listen unless we give them a reason to ask what makes our lives different. We have to stand out and make people wonder. We have to be Good News in the world.

Compassion and true, gritty love are in short supply. We can all do things that seem small, but make a big difference to people. Take time to talk to the homeless man or the Big Issue seller. Find out their story. Stick up for the woman being intimidated by her partner on the street. That woman at work who's always exhausted? Offer to make a meal for her family. Start with the smallest things and people will notice – and wonder why.

'The Spirit of the Sovereign Lord is on me, because the Lord has anointed me to preach good news to the poor. He has sent me to bind up the broken-hearted, to proclaim freedom for the captives and release from darkness for the prisoners' (Isaiah 61:1).

*Name and some details changed to protect Emma's identity

Ben Cooley works for Hope for Justice, an anti-human trafficking organisation. Find out more at www.hopeforjustice.org.uk

THE GOOD LIFE, GOD'S WAY

Rachel Jordan puts on 'God glasses' for a fresh perspective on life

People all have a habit of trying to live life the way they think is best and none of us is perfect. We all make mistakes, get things wrong and many of us feel that we would like to be better people. However lots of people think they are not that bad. In fact, being good isn't really very trendy; being a little bad is seen as the way to live. Be a little naughty, just as long as you don't hurt others. Do what you can get away with!

It may help to ask people whether they think there are any codes or principles to live by. Some people have their own codes and it is always worth asking what these are. Find out how close they are to God's code for living: God's code is summed up in the Ten Commandments. We can then explain that the universe was designed with a code for living; a code for living to make life the best it could be for all people. That code is often still accepted by those who have heard about it. Even those who have never heard of the Ten Commandments will come up with something like them if we ask people what rules they think would work in society. We can then explain that the being who first devised the code was God.

The first Commandment is all about knowing, loving and following God and his code for life. The problem with the human race is that when we follow our own wisdom and our own way in this life we reject God and his ways. We then break the very first and most important code for living (Romans 3:10).

What might help people is to explain that the God who created the code, works in the world now by his Spirit, and listening to the Spirit is

a bit like trying on 'God glasses'. When we put on 'God glasses' we see another dimension to the world; it changes our perception. We see ourselves how we really are; we see all wrong-doing as really wrong. We suddenly see how very extreme the standards of God are: there are no acceptable little bits of wrong. With 'God glasses' on things become either dark or light, there is no acceptable grey. We call all the wrong things we have done sin.

When God's Spirit comes and touches our lives, it is as if he gives us glasses to see what we are really like and that is when we understand our situation.

The worst part of the code is this: when we do something wrong then that needs to be paid for, like breaking an object in a shop; like being charged a penalty for breaking a law - there is a bill that someone has to pay. The problem is that the penalty for wrong doing is to live in darkness away from God, as God cannot be contaminated by our wrong. It is like we collect all these bills and they cling to us and separate us from God. The only way to get rid of people who live a wrong life, which is all of us, would be for us to die forever. That is the code laid down in the universe. When we do things wrong we need to pay for them (Romans 6:23a).

A good question to ask someone you are talking with is whether they have ever felt guilty for something they have done? Have they ever regretted something they have done? What did that feel like? Did they want to do something to put it right?

God needed to remove the wrong and the darkness from us because he loved us and

wanted us to live with him forever but to do this he had to pay the bill.

This could only be done if someone was willing to take our wrong and absorb it, and then stand in the darkness removed from God, paying the price or picking up the bill for it all. So God came himself as Jesus to pay the cost of the wrong. Jesus chose to die on the cross. He paid for all the wrong we had done. He gave up his life. It was like picking up the tab for the worst and biggest bill in the universe and the price on that bill was death forever! (Romans 8:3-4)

Jesus died instead of us. His death means God can forgive us for all the wrong we have done and we are let off free because he paid the penalty. All we need to do is say sorry and ask God to forgive us. That is amazing! (1 John 1:9)

That means we can walk, talk and relate to God in his light. We can be guilt-free, forgiven people. The weight of the wrong things can all be removed by Jesus if we ask him. We can be part of the family of God now and forever (Romans 6:23b). That is the amazing outcome of what Jesus did when he died, instead of us, on the cross.

Dr Rachel Jordan is the National Mission and Evangelism Adviser for the Church of England. She lives in London and is part of a missional community; a group of people who try to live with a shared life and purpose. She is part of the HOPE leadership team.

GOD'S DONE IT ALL!

Religion tells us that we have to DO something for God. Robin Thomson and Kevin Wren explain the good news

'So what do you do?' It's one of the first questions we ask when meeting new people – usually looking for possible areas of common interest. What we do is part of our identity. It can be a mark of our abilities and talents. For some it's also a mark of our financial and social worth. People without paid jobs, for whatever reason, can feel they are not valued.

What we do may also be very important in our relationship with God: 'What must I do to obtain God's favour or reach God's standard?'

People of all religious backgrounds go to great lengths to establish their status with God. They go on pilgrimages or fast; they give to the poor or perform penances. They may be driven by the law of karma, or anxious to balance their good deeds against their bad for the Day of Judgement.

Remember Maria in *The Sound of Music*? She wonders what she has done to deserve such happiness:

Nothing comes from nothing; nothing ever could.

So somewhere in my childhood, somewhere in my youth, I must have done something good.

The trouble with this is that none of us is good enough for God. The apostle Paul pointed out 'There is no one righteous, not even one… there is no one who seeks God…' (Romans 3:10-11). He concluded 'All have sinned and fall short of the glory of God' (Romans 3:23).

God's standard is perfect. None of us has reached it, or can reach it. Jesus said that even

if we haven't done anything bad, our inner thoughts and motives are the same as actions. A successful business executive and a failed labourer may both be offended by another person. One retaliates by knocking him down. The other just takes note and resolves to find a way to humiliate him. What is the difference between them?

The bad news is that none of us can reach God's standard. The good news is that God himself has reached down to us. Paul goes on to say that we are 'justified freely by his grace through the redemption that came by Christ Jesus. God presented Christ as a sacrifice of atonement, through the shedding of his blood – to be received by faith' (Romans 3:24-25).

Jesus' death on the cross has done it all! There is nothing for us to do in order to achieve God's standard.

Can that really be true? In this carefully worded statement Paul uses illustrations from different parts of life to show what Jesus' death on the cross has achieved:

- From the law courts: we are acquitted, declared 'not guilty' (justified). The penalty for our sin and failure has been paid.
- From the marketplace: we have been bought, like slaves in those days, and released (redeemed), set free from the power that sin had over us.
- From the temple sacrifices: an offering has been made which averts God's displeasure at our sin. God himself has provided the offering and removed our guilt.

And all this is given to us as a gift! We simply receive it. We acknowledge that by ourselves we cannot reach God's standard and we hold out empty hands to receive his gift.

'So what do you do - in order to receive God's favour?' The only answer is 'Nothing'.

When businessman and entrepreneur Ram Gidoomal first heard about Jesus' death and the offer of forgiveness, it seemed impossible. He was struggling with the load of his karma:

'How could I ever pay this debt? I knew I was spiritually bankrupt. But I came to realise that either I would have to give up and hope for a better chance to pay it off in the next life, or believe that Christ really had paid for all my sins. I realised that no other guru had claimed to have paid for my karmic debt (paid for my sins), only Jesus. I got on my knees and prayed for Jesus to come in and take control of my life.'

Religion tells us that we have to DO something for God. The good news of the Christian gospel is that it has all been DONE for us through Jesus' death on the cross.

What gives me value? Where is my identity and my worth? It's nothing that I have done for God. But the fact that he has done so much for me gives me infinite value and worth. Now I want to give my whole life in response.

Robin Thomson and Kevin Wren are part of South Asian Concern, a Christian charity with a vision to see South Asians become disciples of Jesus Christ. www.southasianconcern.org

PSST... PASS IT ON!

What makes the Good News, good for you?
asks Peterborough chaplain Chris Duffett

I used to always give them a wide birth. Occasionally I would even cross over the street to avoid them. If I had the misfortune of catching their eye I would smile politely and mumble words like 'in a hurry' or 'no time' and march past like some kind of Olympian speed walker! What do you do when you see a 'chugger' in your local high street? Do you know who I mean? They are the charity workers with a clip board in hand who ask you for financial support.

Now I don't ignore them all the time and when I can, I offer them a listening ear. But first I have to get past their pitch and the script of why I should sign up to support whatever charity they are representing. What I have noticed is that their pitches rarely have life and enthusiasm. Why? Because they have said the same thing over and over, and it has lost its meaning. The message has become boring.

If we try to make the gospel a script, a set of points to remember, it too can become like a product to those who hear what we have to say. How can we communicate our faith in a way that is real and not like a sales patter or a polished presentation?

What makes the good news good to you? As followers of Jesus we need to take time to think through the benefits of being a Christian. May I encourage you to do that today for 10 minutes or so? We often forget what makes our Christian lives good. Subsequently, the Good News becomes 'alright news' or 'nice news' or 'no news'. Yet what we have is the best; it is the news that everyone needs and we are the only ones who will deliver it!

Pass the peace

What is it about the Good News that you could give away? Let me explain what I mean through an awkward moment in my job recently:

As part of my role as city centre chaplain I spent time getting to know people in the market in Peterborough. One day I heard an unusual sound: 'Psst.'

I looked around: 'Psst...'

The noise came from a stall that wasn't selling snakes, so I guessed someone was trying to get my attention. 'Psst...'

I saw a guy behind a pile of handbags on a stall. As I approached he asked, 'Got any hash?'

'Pardon?' I said with embarrassment.

'Mate, got any hash?' He replied urgently. And for some reason tapping my pockets to show that they were empty I apologised for not having any for him! (As if I should carry drugs with me for such occasions!)

I then explained that he didn't really need any drugs and that what he really needed was Shalom from God. I also explained that I was a Baptist minister. He thought it was hilarious that he had just asked a 'man of the cloth' for some drugs!

He then said, 'Well, if I had Shalom I really wouldn't need hash would I!' Without really thinking I asked, 'Would you like some Shalom?'

'Yes please.'

I reached into my bag and, as if I was handing over a precious gift, I said: 'Peace be with you'. Right there and then the man experienced something of God's presence, and with a smile on his face he shared how he felt so much better. We spoke briefly about the love of God and the gift of his Son Jesus. I was able to give away what I had: peace.

The challenge

1. What you and I have as Christians is good, so take time to think what your top three good things are about being a Christian. Write them down, compare them with fellow Christians and what they feel is good about our faith.

2. Consider how you might share that good news with someone who hasn't got a clue what it means to be a Christian.

3. If you feel able to, pray that in the next day or two someone will ask you why you are a Christian, or why you are 'religious'. I Peter 3:15 challenges us always to be prepared to give the reason for the hope that we have. How could you communicate your top three 'good things' to your friends and family in a way that they may understand?

Chris Duffett, a past President of the Baptist Union, is a street evangelist and artist who founded the Light Project, a growing network of people who demonstrate the Christian message and train others in theology and evangelism. www.lightproject.org.uk

Photo: Allen.G / Shutterstock.com

NEW LIFE

Andy Frost uses the symbol of Christian baptism to explain the gospel

The Christian faith is rich in symbols that help us explain the gospel message. Baptism in particular, is packed full of meaning. Many people know what baptism looks like but have not understood what it is about.

When somebody asks you about your faith, you might like to explain what baptism means. If you have been baptised, or christened and confirmed, you might like to explain what took place and why you did it. Here are three points to help you explain what this ancient ritual communicates.

Identity
You were created in the image of God! You are no mistake. However, our identity has been corrupted. You could explain this in terms of:

- Lies – things are spoken over our lives and we believe them. Things like, 'you will never amount to much'. So often we are what others have spoken over us.

- Roles – we find our identity in what we do, in our work or our role in society. But when circumstances change, we can feel that we have lost who we are.

- Doing – we have all made mistakes and failed to live up to the identity that we were created to have. We have put ourselves first and hurt others.

Goodbye
Jesus wants us to rediscover our true identity, as children of God. Baptism symbolises what is happening spiritually - we are dead to the past. Jesus died to get rid of all the lies spoken over us. He died to show us that we are defined by more than the roles we have. He died to get rid of all the mistakes that we have made. We say goodbye to our corrupted identity.

Welcome
In baptism we are symbolically washed clean. We are reminded that as Jesus rose from the dead, we have the same power at work in our lives. We step into a new life, into our real identity. At our core, we are no longer defined by what others say, or the roles we have, or the things we do. Instead we are defined by who God sees us as being. We welcome a new resurrection life with him. Death has been defeated.

Andy Frost is Director of Share Jesus International and Mission Director of Crossing London. He tweets @andythefrosty

SPARKING CURIOSITY

David invited some work colleagues to his baptism. He was amazed when some of them came, and even more amazed when one of them asked for a Bible. David has changed jobs, but still prays for those people.

IT'S MY STORY

Don't preach... start a conversation, says Roy Crowne

We are fascinated by people's stories: Facebook, Twitter, text messaging – even the most mundane facts provoke people's interest. It confirms to me the fact that we were made for relationship. Intrinsic to our value and meaning as human beings, is the desire for relationship that God has placed within us. Everybody has a story. The stories may change in grammar, anecdotes, or visual description, but stories fascinate us.

So, when we come to talk about sharing our faith, our story is essential. Each story is unique, so whether you're shy, confident, introvert or extrovert, you need to be yourself when you tell your story.

Your faith story can be the basis of communicating the gospel. My story is not something where historically I prayed a prayer to Jesus, but rather my story is God's involvement in my life today. It started when I prayed a prayer, but people need to know what God is doing now. Mission, evangelism and sharing your faith flow out of your story.

The best way to describe this is with three circles that connect in the middle, so God's story, my story and their story overlap. We are not preaching, but starting a conversation on a journey with people, as their lives connect with my story and with God's story in relationship.

So often, when we point people to God, we move into propositional truth, to lecture or to preach, rather than simply telling the Jesus story. It's important to recognise that our lives are connected to a bigger story, one that brings perspective to everything we do; this is the story of God. The Bible is THE mega story.

Telling the Jesus story is not for a specialist team, or for a certain type of person, but for each one of us. We tend to make this an individual matter; we do corporate worship and church together but we see our faith-sharing as individual. Let's encourage and be accountable to one another and do this together. Evangelism is not only a personal matter but a part of our corporate worship of Jesus.

Roy Crowne is Executive Director of HOPE.

ALWAYS BE PREPARED

A home group spent time learning to share their faith naturally and confidently by practising three-minute testimonies on each other: one minute 'before Christ', one minute 'finding Christ' and one minute on what God is doing now. Bill and Jean, a couple in the group, then went on holiday and realised that the people on the table next to them were talking about God, but were obviously not yet Christians. The woman turned to Jean and asked for the salt, so Jean took her courage in both hands and asked if they could join the conversation. Bill and Jean shared their faith without embarrassment, remembering what had been learned in their home group.

'Be ready to speak up and tell anyone who asks why you're living the way you are, and always with the utmost courtesy' (1 Peter 3:15 from *The Message*).

GOOD NEWS VALUES

Laurence Singlehurst translates the Good News for today's world

The gospel message is 'good news' – for all time! In the 1600s people were afraid of hell, so a Christian message about avoiding hell was good news. In the 1950s when people still had a Christian moral framework but felt guilty, the message of forgiveness was good news.

Today we hear people talking about values. They know we need some all-encompassing principles to hold our world together. Values, ethics, the Big Society, are seen as important.

The Christian message has at its heart the most spectacular, revolutionary, life-changing set of values. When asked about the Commandments, Jesus said: 'The most important one is this: "Hear, O Israel: the Lord our God, the Lord is one. Love the Lord your God with all your heart and with all your soul and with all your mind and with all your strength." The second is this: "Love your neighbour as yourself"' (Mark 12:28-31).

In this short statement there are four dynamic values.

Firstly, a high view of God. God is good and loving, and when we understand God in these terms it shapes the way we live and influences everything we do.

Secondly, a high value of people. Every individual on earth has value and is made in the image of God. Our world would be a better place if this value was in everybody's heart: marriages would be better; children would be safer; the hungry would be fed - this is good news!

Thirdly, a high value of oneself. We are to love our neighbours as ourselves. How we think about ourselves is really significant today. Psychologists, psychiatrists and sociologists frequently point out that many people's lives are blighted by low self-image. We have good news. You are not who your background says you are, who your teacher says you are; you are not a product of your body-shape or anything else. You have value because you are created in the image of God. Every human has value because Jesus died for each one. More good news!

The final value is sacrificial love. Christian love is demonstrated in the life of Jesus. The *Daily Mail* once ran a headline 'Greed, the New Religion' but as Christians we want to proclaim that life is not about meeting personal needs. It is about loving people sacrificially. To love sacrificially is to act kindly when we would like to be mean, to listen when we would like to talk, to care when we would like to walk away. This sacrificial love is good news.

When we put the gospel in this kind of language we speak something that is relevant and powerful.

Laurence Singlehurst is Director of Cell UK, and a member of the HOPE leadership team.

> What Christian value makes most difference to your life? Print a relevant Bible verse on a business card so you can pass it on when values come up in conversation.

TOGETHERNESS IN A BROKEN WORLD

Rachel Jordan on sharing Christian life in community

The community I am a part of is led by Shannon Hopkins, who came as a missionary to the UK from America. She knew she had to re-learn how to do mission and evangelism in a British urban young adult context. Over time she gathered together a community of people interested in initiating and leading social justice projects. The more projects, the more people joined.

This group is made up of committed Christians, non-Christians and others who have given up on church and aren't sure what they believe. There are around 20 in the core group who live mostly in the East End of London.

Shannon's flat was always a hub for the community but it grew too small, so I decided it was time to move! I could get a two bedroom flat for us both to live in and a space for the community - one which at least 20 people could gather in! It was a long search but God was faithful and after a year, a warehouse conversion flat turned up! I finally moved into a new home to fulfil a specific calling to community living and missional hospitality.

We now have a hub. I am never certain who will be in my home when I get home, or who will be cooking in the kitchen. It does feel like the flat belongs to many of us: a gift from God for shared living. Here around the meal table or hanging about on the sofas after a meal we share life. People of no faith ask questions of faith and slowly seek deeper and deeper answers to their questions. These questions come up in response to sharing Christian life and community.

Sometimes this is scary as a Christian. You know that you are watched: your behaviour, your attitude, your reactions are what are shaping others' understanding of who Jesus is. In many ways it is like a family. We are making disciples in the same way a family makes disciples. It isn't just what we say that has an impact, it is how we live. When we fail we cannot do this in secret. Yet sharing ourselves means that people see we are real and authentic; they get close enough to know who we truly are.

In this context we pray for each other, we bless the food that we eat, and those of no faith respect that. Some have watched and observed prayer, others have even joined in for the first time! It is so amazing as we watch people move closer and closer to Jesus by just being with us!

Dr Rachel Jordan is the National Mission and Evangelism Adviser for the Church of England.

Don't underestimate how much Christian community life communicates. It's powerful!

'The Word became flesh and blood, and moved into the neighbourhood' (John 1:14 *The Message*)

INCARNATE GOD

Our lives may be the only 'translation' of the incarnated Word that our friends and neighbours see, says Ann Holt

One of the most powerful chapters in the Bible is the first chapter of John's Gospel. It describes the most pivotal act in history. In the words of Eugene Peterson's *Message* translation of John 1:14 'The Word became flesh and blood and moved into the neighbourhood'. This act spoke 'salvation into existence'.

The God who up to this point had revealed himself in creation and his dealings with his chosen people, Israel, was now embarking upon his greatest act of love towards the world as a whole. He was taking on human form in the person of his Son, Jesus, who spent his time on earth demonstrating and teaching God's love.

This culminated in the greatest loving act of all when he went to his death on the cross, then to be raised from the dead, which is the very heart of God's plan to restore the whole of his creation to himself. 'It is about the full meaning of everything he was and is and did' (Tom Wright).

From the virgin birth to the resurrection of Jesus, this is a remarkable story and set of events. There is nothing else like it in history. Despite all the attempts to explain it and often to explain it away…

'... the incarnation and resurrection forced themselves upon the mind of the church against the grain of people's convictions... they took root within the church only through a seismic restructuring of religious and intellectual belief' (Tom Torrance).

They never fail to capture the imagination of our communities every Christmas and Easter.

When it comes to sharing Jesus, we must never neglect to tell this story as vividly as possible, encapsulating the mystery as well as the reality and the meaning of it. Taking our friends and family to carol services, performances of The Messiah and Passion Play such as those put on by Wintershall, are all excellent ways of beginning to infuse hearts and minds with the wonder of the incarnation.

This grand story then needs to connect with our own story. Yes we are in it too! God coming to us in bodily form brought about an entirely different possibility of a relationship with him. By experiencing his love for ourselves and allowing him to breathe into us that same Spirit that brought him to life, we can carry that story forward.

In his first epistle John makes acceptance that Jesus is God come in the flesh the ultimate test of Christian authenticity, of real union between the human and the divine, of salvation! 'Every spirit that acknowledges that Jesus Christ has come in the flesh is from God' (1 John 4:2). With such a confession our bodies can become temples of the Holy Spirit. We can become an extension of that incarnation presence in our neighbourhoods. We are called to speak and live his word 'love' in the world. Our faith is to be lived, not just preached. Communication is not just words. 'Don't speak of love, show me' goes the popular song and so does the Bible.

'No one has ever seen God; if we love one another, God lives in us, and his love is perfected in us' (1 John 4:12).

The incarnational presence of God is not just about acts of kindness and living lives of integrity, although it includes those. It is about demonstrating how God is not only restoring individuals, if we will let him, but whole communities and every sphere of life. That same Spirit that empowered Jesus throughout his life, death and resurrection is now available to us, and wants to inhabit us so that we can live transformed, godly, abundant lives. The church represents the body of Christ on earth today. In the words of Archbishop Romero 'We are not messiahs but we are ministers of God's grace.'

Our lives may be the only 'translation' of the incarnated Word that our friends and neighbours are currently seeing. We need to practise the presence of God in every area of life. Our culture is much more interested in whether something works than if it is true, so what manner of love are we showing?

To share our faith in the incarnation and to do it incarnationally we must be prepared to:

- tell the story of the incarnation and its impact on our own story

- answer the big questions about the meaning of the incarnation, while acknowledging the mystery of how it came about

- use drama, music, poetry, signs and symbols to capture the imagination as well as the intellect

- live life as part of the body of Christ which mirrors the one who came and lived among us, living the most abundant life

Canon Dr Ann Holt OBE has worked at Bible Society for over 10 years where she has followed her passion to make the Bible heard in the public square. She attends Malmesbury Abbey and is a lay canon of Bristol Cathedral. She is a member of the HOPE leadership team.

FOCUS ON JESUS

As a young hippie in the 1970s, Laurence Singlehurst stumbled on a secret…

The hippies of the 1970s were in some ways a prototype of postmodern young people today. They embraced the values of 'if it feels good, do it' and they had very definitely walked away from Christian values. But in the late '60s and early '70s there were a significant number of people who came to faith as a result of what was called The Jesus Movement. What interested these people was the life of Jesus. I know this because I was such a young person. I arrived in Australia as a young man focused on having a good time. I had no particular Christian background but I bumped into Christians and what impacted me was Jesus.

In thinking how we communicate the Christian message in our postmodern world, sometimes we miss the obvious. Is the best kept secret of the Christian faith Jesus himself?

In today's context, if we are asking people to become Christians, we are asking them to follow Jesus. But if you talk to people under the age of 45 you will find that they know very little about Jesus: what he did, where he lived, what he said.

So here is a suggestion: Think of three New Testament stories about Jesus, either things that he did or said, or stories that he told; stories that have had a real impact on you. Then when you are asked about the Christian faith you can tell a Jesus story.

Why is this helpful? Firstly, because the story has moved you, when you share it will carry emotional authenticity. Secondly, because you are telling a story you will not use religious language. Most of the stories about Jesus' life, the things he did and said, don't have religious words in them. Thirdly and most importantly, it is all about Jesus. A growing number of theologians are becoming convinced that in our secular, postmodern world, Jesus is the message that we ought to be communicating today.

If this is true then we want to encourage our church members to think of three or four stories that have touched them from the life of Jesus. Maybe it is Zacchaeus up the tree; the woman at the well; the woman caught in adultery; the Sermon on the Mount…. This Jesus-centred approach is, I believe, distinctive and relevant for today.

Laurence Singlehurst is Director of Cell UK, and a member of the HOPE leadership team.

TELLING THE STORY OF JESUS

Paul Langham lets Jesus tell his own story in Who? *a retelling of the synoptic Gospel accounts of Jesus' life*

Copies of *Who? – The Story of Jesus* are available from www.biblesociety.org.uk

I wrote *Who?* for people who don't read the Bible. Many imagine it's boring, untrue, and irrelevant, or even repressive, all about rules and regulations designed to stop us enjoying life.

But those who met Jesus were changed forever by their encounter. Some of them wrote about their experiences and I've tried to imagine how those who wrote about him might tell their stories today. I've blended the accounts from Matthew, Mark and Luke into one single life of Jesus. They pose the question which seems to have been on the lips of everyone who met him, whether follower or opponent – just who is this man?

My aim is the same as theirs – to introduce people to Jesus, whether for the very first time, or in a fresh way. Millions of people today are still claiming to meet him, despite the fact that he was executed over 2000 years ago in one of the most barbaric ways ever devised. If it's possible that the claims Jesus made are true, it must be worth finding out why he still exercises such a powerful fascination.

Jesus invited people into what he called 'God's kingdom'. Unlike any worldly kingdom, it's made up of those who place their faith in him and seek to follow him. Jesus' original followers believed that his death made it possible for anyone who trusts him to live forever with God.

Sounds unbelievable? Well, you will have to make up your own mind, but the original writers all accepted death rather than retract what they believed. Day by day, people just like you and me all around the world are finding that Jesus' invitation is as fresh today as it ever was.

Paul Langham, author of Who? – The Story of Jesus, *is Vicar of Christchurch, Clifton (Bristol) whose passion is both for the Bible and for those who know neither the Bible nor Jesus.*

CHECKING OUT THE BIBLE

Frances was very spiritual in a New Age/occultic sort of way. When she met some Christians who believed the Bible, she decided to check it out. She bought a Bible and a copy of John Stott's book *Basic Christianity* which included a prayer Frances prayed: 'God, if you exist, and I don't know if you do, and if you can hear me, and I don't know if you can, prove to me that you are the God of the Bible, and I will give you my life.'

Over the next three or so years, Frances attended a local church, paying particular attention to the prayer meeting, on the basis that that's where the action should be. She saw God heal people and provide miraculously in answer to prayer. After three years there was a moment when God made his presence felt and said, in effect, 'Make your mind up!' She said 'OK God, you win.' That was 36 years ago and she is still following Jesus.

GOOD NEWS IN PARABLES

Marty Woods — on the look-out for stories to touch hearts

It's not enough to *speak* the gospel clearly. For our friends and neighbours to understand they must also *hear* the gospel clearly.

Jesus' preferred form of public communication was the parable. By telling parables he disclosed 'things hidden since the creation of the world' (Matthew 13:34-35). He said, 'You've been given insight into God's kingdom - you know how it works. But to those who can't see it yet, *everything comes in stories, creating readiness, nudging them toward receptive insight*' (Mark 4:10-12 *The Message*).

Today, gospel communication is hindered by what Ronald Johnstone calls the 'pre-utterance factor'. Because of past encounters with a Christian or a Christian organisation, many people believe they already know the Christian message. Parables drawn from the heart of people's own culture can help overcome wrong perceptions.

Jesus' parables had a way of getting under people's guard. He used familiar truths in ways that reshaped the very way they thought. It's a mistake to see parables as 'bait on the hook'. If we see parables as a clever trick to share the gospel, we have missed the point. Parables respect the history, setting and uniqueness of the hearer. Their impact can lie dormant like a seed awaiting further life-giving conditions.

In Australia, Fusion Youth and Community has developed two 'Aussie' parables that are shared from the front and in one-to-one conversations at Open Crowd Festivals. They are the story of Granny Smith and how she grew the first green apple and the story, known to every Australian, of a World War I hero, Simpson and his donkey. To read these parables go to:
www.opencrowdfestivals.com/parables

What parables communicate the gospel in our culture? Epic films like *Gladiator, The Lord of the Rings, Braveheart, Star Wars, Titanic* or children's stories like *Cinderella, Beauty & The Beast* or *Snow White*, echo the gospel story of love, adventure, heroism and sacrifice. What story or metaphor could you use to explain, as Jesus did, what the kingdom of heaven is like?

Marty Woods is the European coordinator of Fusion Youth and Community. His passion is helping people hear the Good News in their own heart language.

HOLY GROUND

Our first task in approaching another people, another culture, another religion, is to take off our shoes, for the place we are approaching is holy. Else we may find ourselves treading on men's dreams. More serious still, we may forget that God was here before our arrival.

Max Warren, General Secretary of the Church Mission Society.

SHARING FAITH THE JESUS WAY

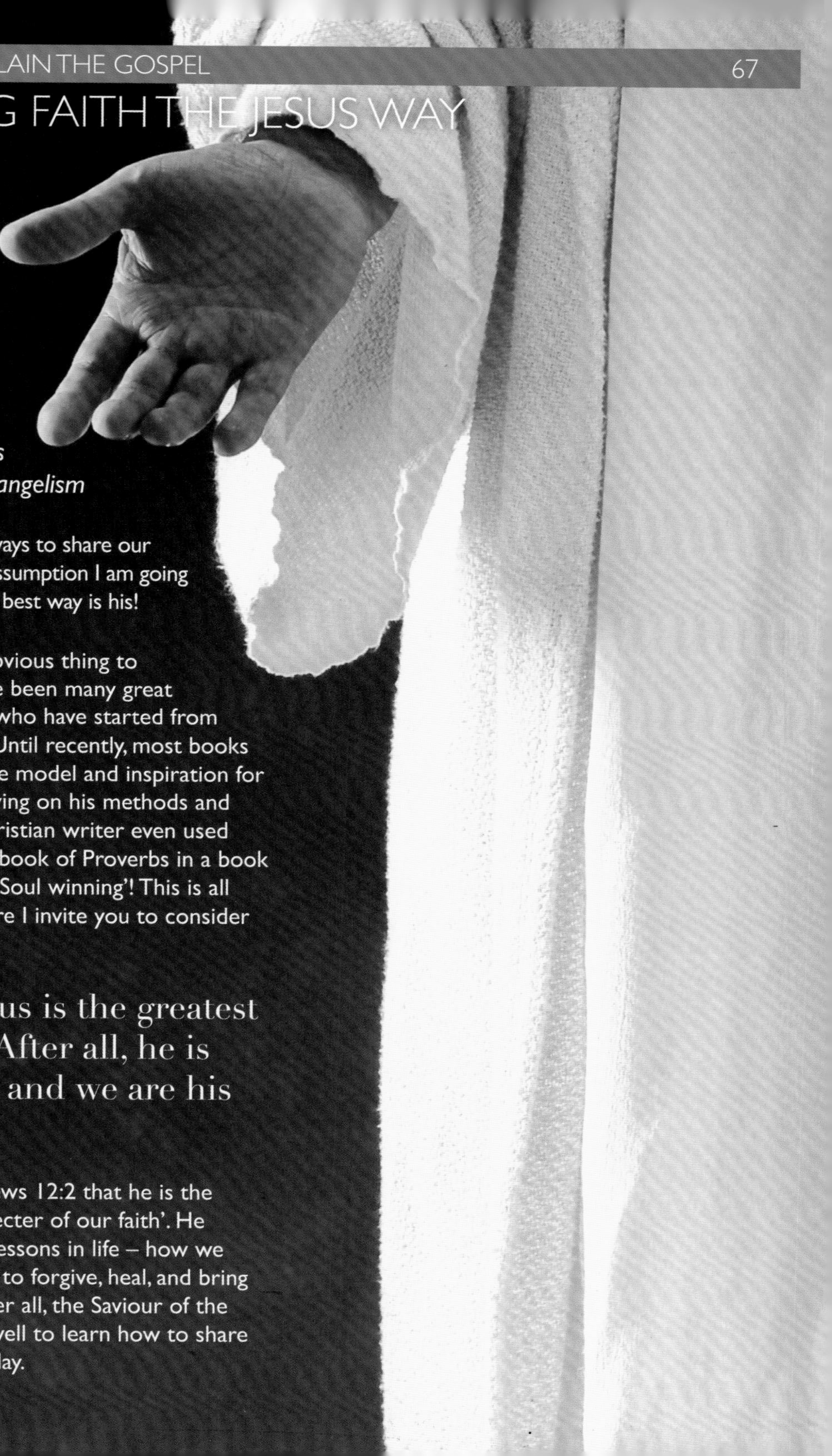

Jim Currin
points to Jesus as
the model for evangelism

There are lots of ways to share our
faith in Jesus. The assumption I am going
to make is this: the best way is his!

This may be an obvious thing to
say, but there have been many great
Christian people who have started from
a different place. Until recently, most books
took St Paul as the model and inspiration for
faith-sharing, drawing on his methods and
message. One Christian writer even used
Solomon and the book of Proverbs in a book
called 'Solomonic Soul winning'! This is all
great stuff, but here I invite you to consider
Jesus and his way.

For me, Jesus is the greatest
evangelist. After all, he is
the teacher and we are his
disciples.

We read in Hebrews 12:2 that he is the
'pioneer and perfecter of our faith'. He
teaches the best lessons in life – how we
treat people, how to forgive, heal, and bring
new life. He is, after all, the Saviour of the
world, so we do well to learn how to share
faith from him today.

My whole approach to sharing faith changed after considering the 'Jesus way' in this short reading from John Taylor's *Mission as Dialogue*.

'An essentially biblical emphasis — all too often ignored by the church — is that Christ is Lord and Saviour of the whole of a person, or he is no saviour at all. Because Jesus insisted on seeing the person whole, one could never be sure which aspect of a person's need he would tackle first. Here comes the paralysed man, helpless and obviously sick in body. His friends have brought him hoping for a simple cure, and Jesus talks about forgiveness of sins. Here on the other hand comes a clear case of spiritual need, an enquirer asking how to gain eternal life, and Jesus gives him an economic answer, telling him how to give away his goods to the poor. Because ultimately Jesus cannot rest content until all of a person's needs are fully met, it doesn't matter much to him where he starts on the work of salvation.'

Exercise

This is a practical exercise, although at first you might think it academic. Have you ever read the four Gospels? If not, I am going to ask you to do just that — and while you do, jot down the variety of messages Jesus gives to those he calls to follow him. Think of the people he met and what he said to them. Note how two people asked Jesus about 'how to obtain eternal life' and each was given a different answer! (Mark 10:17-21 and Luke 10:25-28).

If you have not got time to read the whole 'Gospel in the Gospel', check out the passages and texts for some people Jesus met. Take six individuals like Matthew, Peter, Zacchaeus, Nicodemus, the 'Woman at the Well', and Martha, as examples (Matthew 9:9; Matthew 4:18; Luke 19:1-9; John 3:1-21; John 4:4-26; John 11:21-27). Where did he start? What did Jesus say to them? Is there a pattern?

Action

Think how Jesus addressed all these people individually and spoke in to their situation. Always loving but often challenging. He was on their case but helped them move on in faith. Now, this is how he invites your friends too.

So, take a random number, say six people you know, and ask yourself what Jesus could say to them to help them discover faith, wholeness, forgiveness and new life in him. Don't beat yourself up for not organising something to share your faith - stop and pray. This will be an adventure for you as well as for them as you take this seriously. It may seem full of contradiction, but instead of thinking you have to learn a script, listen to the Lord and to them as Jesus did. Start where they are and see where he leads.

Prayer

Personally, I have found the biggest hindrance to sharing faith and bringing people to Jesus is the lack of prayer. I am amazed how often prayer somehow spontaneously makes people ask and enquire, or the door opens and I feel free to speak. So, keep praying. Read the Gospels. Discover sharing faith 'the Jesus way'.

Jim Currin is a Church Army Evangelist and currently serves as the Secretary for Evangelisation at Churches Together in England. He has a website www.jesus360.org.uk about the 'Gospel in the Gospels' and his own practical book Sharing Faith the Jesus Way, *(BRF 2011).*

ALPHA

Running Alpha is an adventure of faith and action, says Tim May

Alpha is a series of interactive sessions exploring the Christian faith. Guests get a great welcome normally including food, a short talk and time to discuss what they heard in a small group. At the heart of Alpha is the extraordinary offer we all have - to know Jesus. This is too good not to share. Alpha is about extending this invitation to those who do not have faith, but in a relaxed way that allows people to explore with a group of friends, over a period of time. It is the intersection of hospitality, talk, discussion, time and invitation to pray, that seems to create space where many have found faith in Jesus.

Alpha is for anybody to come as a guest and for anybody to help lead. Not everyone can preach but everyone can have a conversation. Many who finish Alpha, who've not yet found faith, help as hosts on future Alpha. We describe these values as belonging, before believing.

Running Alpha is an adventure of faith and action. It takes guts and hard work to put together an environment where people feel welcome to be real about their questions, but Alpha relies on the space we make for the Holy Spirit to reveal Jesus.

We've created Alpha Builder, a simple way for you to run Alpha according to a design that works for your guests. Alpha Builder is a new tool to help anyone run Alpha, anywhere at any time. In six clicks, Alpha Builder will create your perfect Alpha, giving you everything you need to get going, from the talks, to the videos, to the training. For more details visit www.alpha.org/run

Over 22.5 million people have done Alpha worldwide and the adventure continues and seems ever more important in the UK when we look around at how many people don't know who Jesus is.

Tim May became the head of Alpha UK in 2013 and longs to see a generation come to know Jesus.

WHICH COURSE?

There are several different courses designed to help people explore faith. The *Y Course* www.ycourse.com is an eight week enquirers' courses for people with no knowledge of the Bible or Christian language.

Pilgrim: A Course for the Christian Journey, written by Bishop of Chelmsford, the Rt Revd Stephen Cottrell, Bishop of Sheffield, the Rt Revd Steven Croft, Paula Gooder and Robert Atwell, offers teaching and discipleship resources.

The Methodist Church *Compass* course is an interactive guide and group resource that introduces the Christian faith to those wishing to explore its meaning in greater depth.

Your church or denomination might have a preferred course. The key to people finding faith on any course is normally prayer – whatever the course!

CHRISTIANITY EXPLORED

The aim of the course is to allow Mark's Gospel to speak for itself, says Rico Tice

Christianity Explored helps people meet Jesus in the pages of scripture so that they love, live and tell the Good News. It is an informal seven-week course for people who'd like to investigate Christianity, or just brush up on the basics. Looking at Mark's Gospel, it explores who Jesus is, why he came, and what it means to follow him.

Everyone is welcome - from the most sympathetic Sunday schooler to the convinced atheist; whether you have previous experience of church, Christians and the Bible, or none at all.

Courses come in various shapes and sizes. A typical evening starts with a bite to eat or maybe just a cup of coffee, then there's a chance to look at the Bible and ask any questions that you have. There is a short talk, or the DVD, and then a chance to chat about what you've just heard.

The material is flexible and is now being used in countless different formats: with small groups, one-to-one, in homes, prisons and in schools.

The aim of the course is to allow Mark's Gospel to speak for itself and the Lord Jesus to walk off its pages, with a simplicity of language and ease of use which makes it accessible to a wide range of people.

Telling Your Story

A great way to frame your story is to work out when you understood the identity, mission and call of Jesus. When did you see who Jesus was? When did you see why he came? And when did you see what it means to follow him? Whether you are from a Christian or non-Christian home, these three themes go right to the heart of the gospel's work in your life and it keeps your testimony absolutely Christ-focussed. Then we just have to do our bit, which is to preach Christ (2 Corinthians 4:5) and pray that God will do the miracle and open blind eyes to Jesus (2 Corinthians 4:6).

For what we preach is not ourselves, but Jesus Christ as Lord, and ourselves as your servants for Jesus' sake. For God, who said, 'Let light shine out of darkness,' made his light shine in our hearts to give us the light of the knowledge of God's glory displayed in the face of Christ.

But we have this treasure in jars of clay to show that this all-surpassing power is from God and not from us (2 Corinthians 4:5-7).

Pray your friends will grow spiritually hungry and pray for courage and an opportunity to explain what lies at the very heart of your life.

Rico Tice is Senior Minister (Evangelism) at All Souls Church, Langham Place, the birthplace of Christianity Explored.

EXTENDING AN INVITATION

We need to be people who live by faith rather than fear, says Michael Harvey

Many of us cannot remember the last time we invited someone to church, because we have simply stopped inviting people. One reason might be that we fear someone saying 'no' to our invitation, or perhaps we've asked people before and been disappointed by their response. Why do we give up so easily?

I have heard countless stories from Christians who had to be asked several times before they ever accepted an invitation. We need to learn from the persistence shown in the story of the lost coin (Luke 15:8-10) or the lost sheep (Luke 15:1-7), where true persistence and determination was shown because the thing that was lost was worth searching for. It would also help us to remember that 'success' is doing our bit and inviting someone; we cannot control or claim responsibility for the answer they give. It's OK for someone to say no, the important thing is that they were invited.

Some of us fear that we might spoil a good friendship. We don't ask because we are afraid it will cause irreparable damage, but frankly it is very unlikely that we are going to spoil a true relationship over a simple invitation. And of course there's every chance it might change the relationship for the better! But fear of being rejected can just stop the whole process. I have been rejected hundreds of times and yet I can still take it personally. I have to remind myself that it's not a rejection of me; that person is just not yet ready to come to church.

We need to be people who live by faith rather than fear. Fear stands for false, evidence, appearing, real. Fear

is a thief that steals and destroys but it will only become big if we allow it to grow. We can stop it growing by recognising it; then we can resist and reject it. Our doubts and fears will usually step aside when we make an unyielding commitment to action.

For church members to feel confident in extending invitations, it's also important for church leaders to be clear about seeker-friendly services: tell their members in advance how that service will be delivered so they can feel confident in asking friends.

So let's all take courage and be generous in inviting others to come along to our church activities and services, for by doing so we will reap a rich harvest.

Michael Harvey is Principal Consultant for Back to Church Sunday.

BACK TO CHURCH SUNDAY

Back to Church Sunday is an opportunity to extend an invitation to friends or family and ensure they receive a warm welcome when they come to church. Find out more at www.backtochurch.co.uk

SPIRITUAL DISCIPLINES

Rob Hare suggests some activities to help those beginning to explore a new life with God

Practise the Presence of God

We all live our lives in the presence of God, however most of the time we are simply unaware of it. CS Lewis wrote: 'We may ignore him, but can nowhere evade, the presence of God. The world is crowded with him. He walks everywhere incognito.' This is God's world, full of his presence and yet most of the time we are unaware of him. We are rushed, preoccupied, overwhelmed, multitasking and too fatigued most of the time to be with God.

Practising the presence of God is simply a way of waking up and living in a deeper awareness of his activity in our lives and the world around us. A way of staying connected to God throughout the day.

How?

Begin the day by asking God to be with you, and then offer yourself to God for the day ahead asking for his help in frequently reminding you of his presence. You might like to use something that you do regularly throughout the day such as drinking coffee or tea as a prompt to turn your thoughts to God. Each time you stop to drink, talk to God about what you are doing and invite him to be with you.

Practice of Silence & Solitude

Silence and solitude are a rare experience for us who are so connected, switched on and surrounded by all kinds of entertainment, advertising and white noise. We are constantly surrounded by people and Wi-Fi, Bluetooth and other gadgets mean we are hardly ever silent. Even in times of waiting and rest we check our

phone, post stuff on Facebook, send a Tweet, text friends, watch a film or listen to Spotify. Yet creating silence and solitude is key to finding a deeper life with God. In the Bible we read about Jesus going off in the early hours of the morning to find a place of quiet and time alone with his Father and so must we if we want to connect with God.

How?

If this is new for you, begin with just 10 minutes. You might find it helpful to set an alarm clock – then you won't be worrying about the time! Find somewhere quiet to sit (or walk if you prefer) and intentionally relax and become quiet. Ask God to be with you. As you become quiet you may still hear noises, voices, clocks, other distractions such as your thoughts will jump around to many different things – relax, let the noise go, be with God. You can silently use the phrase 'Be still and know that I am God' if it helps you to focus back on God. Continue to be as still and as quiet as you can be. After 10 minutes, reflect on what the experience of being quiet was like. What did you hear from God? What did you learn about yourself? It's easy to give up and consider this a waste of time – but stick with it, try it regularly throughout the week and see if you become more connected with God, both in the activity and more generally in your life.

Lectio Divina

For the first 1500 years of the church people practised reading and listening to the Bible using a method called Lectio Divina. Lectio isn't the same as studying the Bible, instead it's a reflective way of reading a passage of scripture that invites God to speak to me a particular word or phrase for me in this moment in time. In this way, the Scriptures, inspired by the Spirit of God can come alive to me in a new way. Lectio involves five stages:

1. Silence – slow down, become quiet and invite God to be with you.

2. Lectio – read a passage of scripture. Read slowly and out loud, lingering over the words. When a particular word or phrase resonates or connects with you then pause and consider what God might be saying to you. Don't analyse or make judgements. Listen and wait.

3. Meditate – read it again out loud and listen for any invitation that God is extending to you. Reflect on the importance of the words that God is drawing your attention to.

4. Pray – read the scripture for a third time. Now is the time to come to God in prayer and conversation around the words that resonated with you. There is no right or wrong way here – just talk and respond authentically and truthfully. Talk to God about any feelings or emotions that rise up in you.

5. Rest – allow for some time of quiet to allow the words to sink deeply into your soul.

How?

If this is new for you then start by finding a Bible that is easy to read with contemporary language – perhaps the Contemporary English Version (CEV), New International Version (NIV) or The Message (known as a paraphrase version) – all of these are available from Bible Society or Amazon.

It might help to explore the following scriptures: Matthew 13:1-9 and 18-30; Matthew 14:13-21; Mark 4:35-41; Philippians 2:6-11; Colossians 1:9-23; Psalm 1; Psalm 23

Rob Hare is lyfe and spiritual formation officer for Bible Society. Rob oversees Bible Society's lyfe resources which help people individually and in the context of small groups to discover a deeper life with God through the scriptures and spiritual practices.

MAKE A MEAL OF IT!

Much of Jesus' life is told in the context of meals, says Phil Togwell

Jesus didn't say 'listen to me'; he said 'follow me'. Jesus didn't just send his disciples out with words to say, but with a way of life for others to follow and join in with, a shared life worth living.

'Keep open house; be generous with your lives,' he said. 'By opening up to others, you'll prompt people to open up with God, this generous Father in heaven' (Matthew 5:16, *The Message*).

It's amazing how much of Jesus' life is told in the context of meals. And lots of his parables were about shared-meals and hospitality too. Have a look through Luke's Gospel.

So it's not a surprise, straight after Pentecost, to find the disciples gathering the new-believers

and probably plenty of not-yet-believers into local homes to pray and learn and eat together. Jesus told them to follow him, to share their lives in the way that he'd taught them and shown them, and so that's what they were doing. And so must we.

Share words, by all means. But share life too. And start by sharing meals. (And if you need any more persuading, Jesus promises to be present whenever we do.)

Who will you meet for coffee, or for a beer, or invite round to eat with you this week?

Phil Togwell is married with three daughters and a dog (no cats!). He works with 24-7 Prayer, and leads their Prayer Spaces in Schools ministry. www.prayerspacesinschools.com

MEALS WITH MEANING

Hold a 'dialogue supper' to help seekers to explore the gospel

One of the most effective methods of engaging in evangelism is to invite your friends round for a meal with the explicit purpose of having an after-supper discussion about Christianity. Ideally one or two Christians need to invite about a dozen of their uncommitted friends. An attractive and enjoyable meal is had by all. The dialogue leader has the opportunity to get to know the guests. Preferably everyone then moves

to another room, leaving the washing-up well alone! Coffee is served and then the hosts invite the leader to start the discussion.

If it is well set up, the ensuing dialogue is usually good for a couple of hours during which time the gospel is well-aired, its implications pursued and many objections and misunderstandings are discussed. The guests have a good opportunity to state and explore their views and even the persistently unconverted usually enjoy the evening thoroughly and are grateful for the opportunity to take part.

Discuss the wording of the invitation with the dialogue leader. If the evening has been misrepresented, his or her job could be very difficult! A clear statement about the subject matter is essential. Put the focus on Jesus; not religion, the church or ethics.

Invitations need to be given personally (whether written or verbal) without expecting an immediate reply. People need time to consider whether they really want to come. Reluctant guests can make everyone feel awkward.

However, they must eventually be pressed for a definite decision. It is not unreasonable to expect a definite reply for catering purposes and guests will usually appreciate that. Furthermore an invitation that sounds vague will convey the impression that not much effort is being made and the meal may not be worth having. Men are more likely to respond to an invitation from another man. Many men think religion is 'for the birds'.

Think through your policy on alcohol in advance. Will your friends be likely to bring a bottle? Will they feel ill-at-ease having a nice meal without a glass of wine? Can you provide alcohol-free drinks (including beer and wine) for the stated benefit of clear-headed discussion? Avoid pre-dinner drinks (time is also against this) and keep careful control of the corkscrew. Provide attractive non-alcoholic options.

An experienced dialogue leader will know how to handle the discussion. Start with a short summary of the gospel put across in terms of 'this is what Christians believe - let's discuss it,' rather than 'this is what you should believe'. The questions and discussion are likely to flow easily after a short while. Patience for silent reflection is often necessary at first but if it is too prolonged the host might offer the first question. Make sure that it is a basic question that flows from the gospel summary and that non-Christians are likely to be wanting to ask.

A question about the slaughter of the Canaanites at this stage will be unhelpful! Don't argue with the leader, even if you disagree.

Plan the timing and preferred method of ending the discussion. Some leaders like to 'bring the threads together' but others not. Most would want to recommend further reading. Some prefer to let it end naturally and open-endedly, perhaps even on a down-beat. However, it is nice to finish with a well-timed cup of coffee. Have it ready!

Thought also needs to be given to follow-up and the possibility of offering a Bible study discussion on another occasion. One of the natural advantages of these groups is that the folk invited are friends with whom you have regular contact. Individual follow-up should therefore be fairly easy.

From the Confident Christianity *course — originally assembled by Dr Peter May and Dr Peter Short (both Southampton GPs) for day conferences organised by the Christian Medical Fellowship for medical students.*
www.cmf.org.uk

Here are some problems to avoid:

1. Lack of good friendships with non-Christians who would respond to such an invitation. It may be necessary to invite up to 20 people, for an adequate number of acceptances.

2. Invitations that are unclear as to the nature of the meeting.

3. Inviting people who have nothing in common with each other and are asking very different sorts of questions, so the group doesn't gel.

4. Too many Christians come, with consequent religious in-talk over the meal, and jargon during the dialogue. The fewer Christians the better! Non-Christians will feel more at ease if they sense they are in the majority.

5. Too much time spent over the meal, leaving people too tired or too late to get into the subject matter.

6. Too much alcohol (often brought by gracious guests!).

7. Guests insisting on washing up, or Christian friends doing it too loudly in the next room.

8. Inappropriate contributions from the Christian hosts who haven't grasped the principles of dialogue evangelism and fail to appreciate the experience, skills and 'apologetics' of the leader.

9. Failure to appreciate group dynamics, allowing the discussion to splinter.

10. Failure to put the guests at ease e.g. by saying (or worse, singing!) 'grace', or by attacking guests for their views. The host who thumbs a big black Bible is particularly unnerving!

It should not surprise us that the best things we can do in evangelism require the most care and preparation.

BELONGING BEFORE BELIEVING

Working with Christians on a community project starts the journey to faith for some. Catherine Butcher and Ayo Adedoyin report

Spending time with Christians and doing something together can be the beginning of a journey to believing in Jesus.

Christmas Lunch on Jesus (CLOJ) is an outreach project initiated by Jesus House in London which distributes free Christmas hampers to residents of the most deprived Wards in the London Borough of Barnet. They focus on making sure children and single parents living in deprived conditions can enjoy a Christmas lunch with all the trimmings.

Mollie is one volunteer who got involved because she wanted to help make a difference in someone's life at Christmas. She said: 'The distribution day was amazing! I volunteered with one of the participating churches in Colindale who were very warm and friendly. It was nice to meet and work with new people and the planning and organisation was excellent. The recipients of the hampers were also amazing. One old lady burst into tears when she opened her door to us; it was clear that without this, Christmas wouldn't have happened for her. CLOJ brought it home to me that we all need the love of God; it was a very fulfilling experience.'

Big Lunch

Many church-led community projects involve churches serving and working for their community. Others, like the Big Lunch, are an opportunity to work with businesses and community groups. Again, by doing something together, people who are not-yet-Christians can see Christian values up close in action; relationships are built and there are often opportunities to talk about Jesus. Good deeds create good will and good will is a platform for sharing the good news.

Where do you begin? Start with something you enjoy doing, and do it together with others. If you love watercolour painting, book the church hall to spend evenings painting watercolours with others. Some people, who have enjoyed an art group and the chatter over colour-washes, have gone on to join a Christian discovery course and have become Christians.

A Saturday afternoon, friendly football kick-about might be more to your liking; sports are a great way to get alongside other like-minded people, make friends and share faith.

Catherine Butcher is HOPE's Communications Director; Ayo Adedoyin oversees the Community Action Department and Communications team at Jesus House, London.

LEARNING TO PRAY

Roger Bretherton's exercise for not-yet Christians who want to know how to pray

Here's a quick prayer exercise to have up your sleeve if you're ever in a conversation with someone who'd like to pray but doesn't know how. They can try it as an experiment, it works anywhere, and it goes something like this:

1. Cast your mind over the last 24 hours. What event first springs to mind? It could be happy or sad, wonderful or fearful. But whatever it is, recall it as vividly as you can, and hold it in mind for a moment.

2. Once you have it, ask yourself this question: if there was a kind loving God, and he was speaking to me through this event, what would he be saying?

3. Take some time to settle on a sentence or phrase that sums up what you think a good God would say. Don't be too precious about it. Try a few phrases and settle on the one that has the best feel to it.

4. Then ask yourself this: if God were saying that to me, what would I pray in response? Pray something short. It could be a quick thank-you or a brief request. And when you're done, you may want to say 'Amen'.

Dr Roger Bretherton is Senior Lecturer in Psychology at the University of Lincoln and author of The God Lab: Eight spiritual experiments you can try at home *(Integrity).*

THE PRESSURE'S OFF

Give people freedom to respond on their own, says Laurence Singlehurst

A number of years ago I was involved in some informal research asking how do people make the significant step of faith and commitment? To my surprise, as many as 30% of the people that I spoke to made a commitment in their own private space. This should not have been a surprise – it was my own personal experience. I met Christians, lived in their Christian community for a while, attended their church services and gained some understanding of what following Jesus was all about. But in the end, it was a private moment standing on a street corner where I had an honest and real conversation with God and something significant and wonderful took place.

When we understand that this is a very real possibility, and that British people on the whole can be quite private, then this takes the pressure off feeling that we should always invite people to things (not that this is a bad thing) or push them to make a decision.

We can suggest to people that they should feel free to talk to God in their own time and in their own place. Sometimes it just takes a walk in the woods, a special moment touches people's hearts, they talk to God and wonderful things take place.

Laurence Singlehurst is Director of Cell UK, and a member of the HOPE leadership team.

JOURNEY

Philip Jinadu on seeker-friendly churches

If only churches were more like department stores our evangelism would be a whole lot more effective. The central point of any major department store is the escalator, helping people to journey through the store and get what they're looking for. They are literally structured for seekers.

When a person is on a journey of faith there are different levels they go through. Felt spiritual need, curiosity/intrigue about church, willingness to explore faith, questions to work through, opportunities to respond, integration into community, on-going discipleship and so on. People need to take these steps in their own time. The problem with most churches

is that we expect seekers to do all the work themselves. We can put on great guest events from time to time, but there's no easy next step.

At Woodlands, when people come to our bonfire parties we make sure they're invited to the Christmas specials. At Christmas events, there are flyers for our January Comedy Cabaret. During that, a presentation is made about the term's Alpha course, which is about to start. Not everyone processes through in a nice, neat way, but we work hard to make sure that when people are ready to take their next step, they know where to go.

Philip Jinadu is an Associate Minister at Woodlands Church Bristol. www.woodlandschurch.net

LIVE LIFE 123

Become a disciple who makes disciples, says Matt Summerfield

'Blessed are those…whose hearts are set on pilgrimage' (Psalm 84:5) reminds us that faith is a journey. But how do you make sure you're journeying in the right direction? Answer: you need to be surrounded by people who will help you grow.

- Firstly, we are 'learners' – so we need to be connected to people who are ahead of us in the journey of faith, who can help us become everything God created us to be. Try to find ONE person who can be this for you.

- Secondly, we are 'travellers' – we need to be connected to friends who we share our lives with; mutually accountable, challenging, real relationships. Try to find TWO people who can be this for you, and you for them.

- Thirdly, we are 'teachers' (we all have a story and wisdom we can share with others) - so we need to be committed to grow and develop other people in their faith. Inspiring each of them to share their faith with others. Try to find THREE people who you can help to live like Jesus.

In Matthew 28:18-20 Jesus reminds us that he has given us this incredible privilege to be his disciples who make disciples. If you put the above in place – let's call it LiveLife123 – it will really help you in your journey of faith – AND you'll be good news to others too!

Matt Summerfield is Pastor of Hitchin Christian Centre he also works with Live Life 123, see www. livelife123.org for more help in this area.

NO ONE LIKES LOOKING STUPID

Andy Frost on 'apologetics' — explaining what we believe

When it comes to sharing our faith many of us are concerned that we might get asked a question that we just can't answer, that we might let God down or look stupid.

It's important to prepare ourselves for difficult questions. The word 'apologetics' comes from the Greek legal word apologia. It's a word that was used in court to give a formal explanation in response to accusations. When it comes to sharing our faith, we need to be able to explain why we believe what we believe.

Here are my five top tips when it comes to tackling difficult questions…

1. Get ready…

Are there big questions that you've been asked but haven't thought through? What questions might come up from the people that you talk to about Jesus? For example, when talking with Muslims, questions often come up about the Trinity; scientists often ask questions on Genesis.

This resource gives you an introduction to a handful of the big questions, but there will be other questions that you will come across. On pages 92 and 93 you will find recommended books and websites to allow you to explore more. Don't put it off! Equip yourself and talk through what you discover with others from your church.

2. Questions

Whenever people come to you with difficult questions, it is important to remember that there is often a question behind the question. For example, when somebody quizzes you about hell, it might be because someone they know has just died. Jesus often asked questions of the people who came to him with questions. This is a really helpful thing to do.

3. Winning

Remember, winning the argument is not the most important thing. Jesus spoke truth with grace. Rather than simply winning an argument, leave the person you are talking to open to their next encounter with a Christian.

4. It's okay to say, 'I don't know'

When you are asked difficult questions you might not know what to say. We will never have all the answers. It is OK to say, 'I don't know' then tell the person you are speaking to that you will find some answers to their questions for the next time you meet.

5. Point to Jesus

Sharing our faith is ultimately about sharing Jesus. We can get side tracked into intense conversations about side issues, but keep bringing the conversation back to Jesus. Remember, some people just love a good discussion. It's important to discern whether the conversation really is going anywhere or whether they are just enjoying being argumentative.

Andy Frost is Director of Share Jesus International and Mission Director of Crossing London. He tweets @andythefrosty

A GOD OF LOVE IN A WORLD OF PAIN

Stephen Gaukroger tackles the question of why God allows suffering

The question of suffering boils down to this: how can a God of love let all this suffering go on in his world? Either he doesn't exist at all, or he is a vicious tyrant who enjoys seeing people in pain! This seems to present a pretty strong case against the existence of a loving God, and there certainly is no slick or easy answer to the problem of suffering. But perhaps the answer is more like a jigsaw puzzle, with large pieces that fit together to make a picture. Our confusion at this massive puzzle (how can a loving, powerful God stand by while we suffer?) becomes clearer if we take it one piece at a time.

Jigsaw piece 1

The hard truth is that we have only ourselves to blame for much of the suffering in our world. It's no good blaming God when a drunken driver kills an innocent pedestrian, or when a football hooligan knifes one of your friends on the way home from the match. Both these incidents, and others like them, point the finger at the real culprits - the human race. God can hardly be blamed for suffering we choose to bring on ourselves. Bloodshed in Afghanistan, mass murder in Syria, thousands crushed to death in the Twin Towers terrorist attack of September 11, 2001 - such terrible atrocities replicated around the world reveal the horrifying consequences of man's inhumanity to man. When nations hoard food and refuse to give aid to the hungry, when governments declare war on each other, when gangs terrorise housing estates, when adults sexually abuse children, when old people are robbed and beaten, we are to blame.

Now it is true that we personally may not be to blame for all these problems, but we are personally to blame for some things. No one reading this can honestly say they have never caused anyone any suffering. Never an angry word to your partner or child? Never a selfish action at work? Never a refusal to help someone in need? No, the plain fact is that, to a greater or lesser degree, we all contribute to the suffering in the world.

God could only get rid of the suffering we inflict on ourselves by getting rid of us (pretty drastic!) or by turning us into androids who only acted on his command. Both these options would rob us of freedom of choice. We have been given the privilege of freewill, so we have to live with the consequences of exercising that freedom. Both suffering and joy come from having choice.

Jigsaw piece 2

What about the suffering we don't cause, the things we have no control over - like earthquakes, famine, volcanoes and other natural disasters? Strange as it may seem, even here we must take some responsibility.

Earthquakes have indeed caused death, homelessness and injury on a huge scale. Thousands suffered in major quakes in Mexico in 1985 and in Japan in 1995, for example. What is not as well known is that a vast amount of suffering could have been prevented. As long ago as 1906 earthquakes were monitored and the resulting devastation scrutinised. After the San Francisco earthquake at that time, Dr T Nakamura was sent by the Japanese government to the earthquake zone to assess why there had been such colossal loss of life, injury and devastation In his report this sentence stands out 'Dishonest mortar was responsible for nearly all the earthquake damage.' In other words, the damage could have been drastically reduced by decent, reinforced buildings!

For over 100 years we have known how to minimise earthquake damage, but recent earthquakes reveal how little we put this knowledge into practice.

There are human dimensions to other natural disasters, too. For example, thousands suffered and died in the last century from famine in Africa; but years before it happened, relief organisations were warning governments that famine was coming. All too often corrupt rulers spend millions on lavish premises or military equipment while their people starve. A great deal of pain and suffering could be avoided if governments and individuals acted differently.

It does seem unreasonable to blame God for our own unwillingness as human beings to act responsibly. Disaster after disaster in our

world entails human failure either causing the catastrophe or making it considerably worse. We do have to carry the can for this ourselves. But, having said all that, there is suffering which appears to be beyond our control - natural disasters that strike without warning and seemingly without cause. How can we explain these?

Christians believe that God made a perfect world. Unfortunately, people decided they knew better than God how things ought to be run, and turned their backs on him. This resulted in a rift between God and the human race which, like the fallout after a nuclear accident - also had an effect on creation. A once perfect world became imperfect, and human beings found themselves in alien, hostile territory, surrounded by a natural environment 'red in tooth and claw', infected by sickness and disease. (You can read the full story in the first three chapters of the Bible.) So we are at the mercy of disasters which are symptoms of the malfunction in the relationship between ourselves and our creator.

Jigsaw piece 3

God understands our suffering because he himself has experienced it! No one can accuse God of being an uninvolved deity, just sitting back and watching us suffer. He sent his Son to earth to check it out for himself, to experience first-hand what life was all about for the human race.

Many people find great comfort from the knowledge that God has endured human suffering and understands what we go through. He has been where we are - the chief executive has experience of life on the shop floor, the captain has worked in the engine room, the chief of police has walked the beat. God has been down here at the sharp end.

Jigsaw piece 4

The best treatment for a bleeding wound is a bandage, not a lecture on suffering! When we are suffering, most of us want not clever answers to philosophical questions but practical, down-to-earth help. If we deny the existence of a loving God (by saying he is a figment of our imagination or he exists but won't come to our rescue) we rob ourselves of the major source of relief. If there is no God, everything that happens is a result of chance. Not much comfort there! If he just doesn't care, that's even worse! What a terrible position to be in.

In contrast, Christians believe in a God who can help. Despite many misunderstandings, Christianity is not pie-in-the-sky-when-you-die; it's more like life-right-here-on-the-ground-while-you're-still-around! It's about a relationship with someone who is with us in every difficulty and who promises never to leave us however tough it gets.

In fact, the kind of help God provides isn't easy to beat! And with it comes a guarantee to every Christian that all unanswered questions will one day have answers, all wrongs be put to right, and life will be enjoyed forever without suffering of any kind. This promise has strengthened and encouraged Christians over the centuries. It sounds a fantastic offer, and it is. Be careful not to reject it too quickly. If you dismiss it without thought, what an idiot you would feel one second after you die to discover it was true!

What it adds up to is this. There is a tremendous amount of pain in individual lives. We have been promised help and support in this life and a complete absence of suffering in the next. There is not much else on offer, so we might as well check out what there is pretty carefully.

Stephen Gaukroger, a past President of the Baptist Union, is the Chairman of Crossing London and founder director of Clarion Trust International. www.clariontrust.org.uk

HASN'T SCIENCE DISPROVED GOD?

Science is wonderful at answering the pragmatic questions: what? and how? says Glen Scrivener

Thinking God's Thoughts

When Johannes Kepler discovered the laws of planetary motion in the early 17th century he did not lose his strong Christian faith. Instead he spoke of the wonderful privilege of 'thinking God's thoughts after him'. That's been the mind-set of so many giants in the history of science: Copernicus, Galileo, Newton, Faraday and, in our own day, Christians like Francis Collins, leader of the Human Genome Project. They have not imagined 'a God of the gaps' who was ever shrinking as their science progressed. They have believed in 'the God of the whole' whose thoughts they were thinking after him.

Faith and Foundations

Einstein said, 'The fact that the universe is comprehensible is the greatest miracle.' Science depends entirely upon this 'miracle'.

We need our minds 'in here' to correspond to the world 'out there' and for both of those to correspond to dependable laws of nature 'up above'. The fact that this triangle lines up so perfectly is astonishing. But Christians should not be surprised. Jesus, our Maker, sustains the universe (Hebrews 1:3) and at the same time has entered our world and assumed our humanity (John 1:14). He is the one who unites the laws 'up above', the world 'out there' and our minds 'in here'. Faith, therefore, does not undermine science. Faith in Christ is the strongest possible foundation for scientific enquiry.

Mechanism and Maker

Science is wonderful at discovering mechanisms in nature. But understanding a mechanism does not rule out a maker. If you explain the inner workings of a new contraption, I don't say 'Wonderful, now we can do without the inventor.' Instead I say 'So that's how they did it. Ingenius!' Same with science and God. We love to find out more of the mechanisms, but this should make us exalt our maker, not exclude him!

Pragmatics and Purpose

Professor of Mathematics, John Lennox often asks people to imagine a cake baked by Aunt Mildred. The cake is passed around various scientific departments. They discover 1001 facts about the cake's nutritional content, its chemical and physical properties; they reverse engineer the recipe and replicate its tasty goodness. Wonderful! But can any of the scientists tell you why the cake was baked? No. For that you'd have to ask Aunt Mildred. Science is wonderful at answering the pragmatic questions: what? and how? It is simply not in a position to answer questions of purpose: why?

Evolution and Creation

Christians take different views on the question of evolution but some things we all agree on. Every creationist believes that natural selection happens – after all, from a single pair of cats on the Ark we now have tabbies and tigers. At the same time no Christian evolutionist thinks natural selection explains everything about life. So we can all agree that natural selection happens while questioning its ability to explain the whole show.

For the sake of argument though, let's imagine that random mutations and natural selection account for all the varieties of life on planet earth. This only explains the origin of the species. That's as far as Darwin can take you. He cannot explain the origin of life itself (he must assume the origin of life). He cannot tell you the origin of the cosmos. And he cannot tell you the origin of consciousness. Those three origin questions are far more pressing, yet natural selection is no help for any of them. Science simply does not have a credible mechanism for explaining these deep issues. And even if it did, the mechanism would not disprove the maker.

Glen Scrivener is an Australian evangelist working for Revival Media. His evangelistic website is www.three-two-one.org and he blogs at www.christthetruth.net

One afternoon I was with one of my patients, a wonderful elderly woman who had very bad heart disease and had suffered mightily for it, and for whom we'd essentially run out of options. She had a particularly bad episode of chest pain while I was with her. She got through it, and then explained to me how her faith was the thing that helped her in that situation. She realised that the doctors around her weren't giving her that much help but her faith was.

After she had finished her own very personal description of that faith, she turned to me (I had been silent), looked at me quizzically, and said, 'I've just shared my personal faith in Christ with you, doctor, and I thought you might actually say something but you haven't said anything. What do you believe?'

Nobody had ever asked me that question so directly, and with such a generous, sincere spirit before. I felt the colour rising in my face, and I felt an intense disquiet about even being there. I stammered something about not being quite sure and left the room as fast as I could.

That day at my patient's bedside started a journey for me…

Francis Collins, Former Director of the National Human Genome Research Institute at the National Institutes of Health, Bethesda, Maryland, taken from Test of Faith (Paternoster), which includes contributions from a range of leading scientists including Dr Francis Collins, Prof Alister McGrath, Dr Ard Louis, Dr Jennifer Wiseman, Prof Bill Newsome, Revd Dr John Polkinghorne, Revd Dr Alasdair Coles, Dr Deborah B. Haarsma, Prof Rosalind Picard, Prof John Bryant.

WHY IS GOD SO VIOLENT IN THE OLD TESTAMENT?

Glen Scrivener points to the judge who became our refuge

Confronting the Caricatures

According to the Apostles, the Old Testament is all about 'the good news of peace through Jesus Christ' while the New Testament concerns Christ, 'the Judge of the living and the dead' (Acts 10:36-43). Grace in the Old, Judgement in the New! What unites the Scriptures is Christ himself.

John tells us Christ was there 'in the beginning' (1:1-18). Therefore Christ was the one Moses, Abraham and Isaiah saw and wrote about (5:37-47; 8:56-58; 12:37-41). The problems we might have with 'the God of the Old Testament' we have with Jesus. Having said this...

The Times Have Changed

When Jesus came in the flesh he fulfilled and ended the temporary structures of the Old Testament, in particular the Temple with its priests and sacrifices and the theocratic nation with its kings and armies. Instead Jesus relentlessly urges forgiveness and non-violence (see Matthew 5:38-48; 26:52-54; Luke 6:27-36; John 18:36).

So here's our challenge: Jesus tells us to put down our swords and to pick up his book. Yet in his book (the Old Testament) we read of several holy wars. What to think?

Let's examine the central act of violence brought up in these discussions – the conquest of the Promised Land, commanded in Deuteronomy, fulfilled in Joshua. (For further reading see Paul Copan's Is God a Moral Monster?)

The Conquest of Canaan

For 400 years Canaanite cultures were involved in child-burning and other grotesque evils (Genesis 15:13-16; cf 'Molech', Leviticus 18:21). The Lord gave them centuries to repent of it – considerably longer than any other 'just war' ever launched. He then, through his people, visited them with a one-off, unrepeatable judgement. It had nothing to do with race – this was not genocide. Later on, when the Israelites were also guilty of such sins, they too were judged.

Every Canaanite who ever sought mercy from the Israelites was spared (see Joshua 2 and 9). Certainly, prior to the conquest, God speaks the language of total destruction (Deuteronomy 20:16-18). Yet Copan argues that this was well understood in the day as militaristic hyperbole. The language of 'driving out' precedes and predominates over language of 'wiping out' (Deuteronomy 7:17-24; 9:1-6). And when Joshua sums up his achievements, he considers that he's done what Moses had commanded – this, in spite of the fact the Canaanites were not fully driven out, let alone wiped out (see Joshua 23-24; Judges 1).

Judgement and Grace

Having said this, these stories still shock. God is not a Rotarian. There is blood and fire to this Righteous Judge – in both Testaments. But remember three things:

First, we often complain that God should do more about evil in this world. When he gives us this one-off, unrepeatable picture of his righteous judgement, we cannot then complain at his intervention!

Second, the Bible makes it clear we are all moral and spiritual Canaanites. We all need the mercy shown to Rahab in Joshua 2. This is what Jesus provides, absorbing the fire and justice on the cross and providing us with refuge.

Third, in Jesus we are brought into a realm beyond judgement – a realm of cheek-turning, enemy-forgiving love (Colossians 1:13-14). Thus the New Testament views these ancient wars as types of our own campaign of peace (2 Corinthians 10:1-5; Ephesians 6:10-20). 'Christian violence' is a contradiction in terms.

In the end, the problem of violence does not lie in millennia old Hebrew wars but in our hearts. The solution is not to reject Jesus or his book. The only answer is Jesus himself - the judge who became our refuge.

Glen Scrivener is an Australian evangelist working for Revival Media. His evangelistic website is www.three-two-one.org and he blogs at www.christthetruth.net

CAN WE TRUST THE GOSPELS?

God's word vindicates itself when God himself speaks through it, says Glen Scrivener

The Bible Proves the Bible

The Gospels are not free-floating. They fit into the symphonic story of Scripture. Therefore the way they fit is a wonderful testimony to the truth of the whole Bible. A book like Walter Kaiser's *Messiah in the Old Testament* highlights over 60 detailed Old Testament predictions which Jesus concretely fulfils in the Gospels – these just scratch the surface. Josh McDowell cites 29 Old Testament prophecies that are fulfilled on Good Friday alone. Perhaps take your friend to Genesis 22, Psalm 22 or Isaiah 53 then read Matthew 27 for the fulfilment.

The Gospels Present Themselves as History

Show the enquirer Luke 1:1-4 and see that the authors of the Gospels are not attempting to write fables but history. Look through the early chapters (eg 2:1-4; 3:1-2, 23-38) and see how Luke mentions scores of historical figures and places. This is not 'once upon a time in a land far away'. Luke is doing everything in his power to convey these as real-world, historical events. At that point he's either telling the truth or concocting an elaborate and wicked hoax. What do we think?

Lost in Transmission?

Bart Ehrman wrote a best seller called *Misquoting Jesus*, alleging that today's copies of the Gospels aren't necessarily what the authors first wrote. We have nearly 25,000 ancient manuscript copies of the New Testament – a number that dwarfs anything else in ancient literature. Unsurprisingly, given they were all hand-copied, there are discrepancies. Yet if we were worried that these differences were of any great importance, Ehrman's attempt to make a sensational case should reassure us.

The best he can do is point to Mark 16:9-20; John 8:1-11 and 1 John 5:8 which any decent Bible translation will itself highlight without embarrassment. Then he points out that we have alternative readings for verses like Mark 1:41 and Hebrews 2:9. Your Bible's footnotes will probably tell you the options and you can see for yourself how little hangs on the difference. This is the best case offered by biblical studies' most prominent sceptic. Therefore any fears that the true message of Jesus has been lost are unfounded.

Lost Gospels?

But aren't there many lost Gospels that were suppressed by the church? No, and you should really stop believing Dan Brown! Gospels like The Gospel of Thomas were written at least a century after the original four, in a language Jesus didn't speak, in a completely different style (collections of sayings, not narrative) and proposing concepts of God, salvation, the body and women that are utterly alien to the Bible (and to all good sense). If you want to see why the church always rejected them, just read them.

Defend the Bible?

Charles Spurgeon's famous line is still the best on this subject: 'Defend the Bible? I would as soon defend a lion! Unchain it and it will defend itself.' Our first priority is to get Scripture into people's hands. I always challenge enquirers to pick up a Gospel (perhaps John) and shoot up a prayer: 'Dear God, if you're there, show me the real Jesus.' I tell them 'You've got nothing to lose. If he's not there, he won't answer. But if he is, then you need to meet his Son. This book is the way to do it.'

Of course we can assure enquirers that the Bible is internally consistent, historically accurate, well-attested, faithfully passed down, etc. But none of that makes it the word of God. God's word vindicates itself when God himself speaks through it.

Glen Scrivener is an Australian evangelist working for Revival Media. His evangelistic website is www.three-two-one.org and he blogs at www.christthetruth.net

HOW CAN A GOD OF LOVE SEND PEOPLE TO HELL?

God is in the business of getting people into heaven, says Stephen Gaukroger

Hell means total separation from everything good. The flames described in the Bible may be picture language, but the reality they represent is no figment of the imagination. One of the reasons hell exists is because of the seriousness with which God takes the decisions of men and women. If we choose to reject him, his offer of life and way of escape from all the dirtiness in the world, he refuses to overrule our decision. He won't force us to accept his love – this would rob us of the privilege of choice and make us mere androids. So we have to take the consequences of our decisions. This means that, by choosing to live without God, we have indeed chosen to live without God, now and forever.

It is no use asking why we can't opt to live without God in this life and to live with him in the next. The question completely misses the radical nature of our choice. For instance, suppose we choose not to have any children of our own and then, at the age of 80, change our minds and want to have grown-up children to look after us. By then it's too late. Our earlier decision has inevitable consequences. So it is

with our decision about God. There comes a point (death) when our earlier decision is too far gone to change, which means we have chosen to spend eternity living in the presence of our own sinfulness and in the absence of God.

All this shows that, far from God sending people to hell, they seem to be sending themselves. After all, it would be unreasonable to blame the doctor for my ill health if I refuse to take the medicine he prescribed! The divine doctor has diagnosed the sin-sickness of mankind and offered a forgiveness-cure. If we refuse or ignore the offer, we will have to live with the disease. This is what hell is – living after death with all our worst traits still raging inside us, only now they are unrestrained by God or social convention, a seething mass of unforgiven vices and resolved conflicts. God does not want anyone to go to hell (see 1 Timothy 2:4), so he has prepared a way for the human race to escape its horror. He is in the business of getting people into heaven, not sending them to hell!

Stephen Gaukroger is the Chairman of Crossing London and founder director of Clarion Trust International. www.clariontrust.org.uk

IS JESUS THE ONLY WAY TO GOD?

The gravity of Jesus' claim is shocking, says Michelle Tepper

In John 14:6 Jesus says, 'I am the way, the truth and the life, no one comes to the Father except through me'. Why is it that this verse, which is so central to a correct understanding of the Christian faith, is also one of the verses most difficult for those outside the faith to accept? Often the initial response people have when they hear these words is one of shock or outrage. This reaction shouldn't surprise us really because the gravity of Jesus' claim is shocking. To put it blatantly, it means no one can find God without Jesus. The most common objections that arise in response to this claim can usually be grouped into the following statements or a combination thereof:

1. Christianity should be avoided because it is exclusive.

2. Christians are arrogant for claiming they know the truth.

3. What about all of the people who haven't heard?

When someone's main objection to the Christian faith has to do with exclusivity, it is often helpful to gently point out that all worldviews are implicitly exclusive. Differences can only occur by exclusion, and every religion differs on any number of areas, such as morality, God, eternity, reality etc. In fact, a brief study of the major world religions alone reveals that most of them were born through rejection or 'exclusion' of certain elements of a previous religion. Even 'universal' systems built on total inclusion end up excluding all 'exclusivists'. The truth will always be exclusive.

This leads us to the next common objection: is it arrogant for Christians to say that we

alone know the truth about God? The answer to this question is directly linked to our understanding and explanation of why we are Christians and how we define truth. As Christians we have come to know the truth about God, only through the person of Jesus Christ. We have been saved from an eternity without God, not by any intellectual, experiential or behavioural assent we made to find the truth about him, but because God made himself known to us in history. This is precisely why we are confident that we know the truth about God, because, for the Christian, truth is located not in an idea but a person. Not only should this put an end to any temptation towards arrogance, but also to the accusation of it. When truth is personal, then faith and confidence in the truth is not about a blind intellectual leap but a conscious decision to trust the character and nature of someone who has proven faithful.

This brings us to the root of the final objection people often have about the Christian faith. For many who work through flawed assumptions about exclusivity or arrogance, these answers still leave serious doubt about the character and nature of a God who seems to leave such a narrow path to him. Once again, any conversation on this sensitive and important dilemma must be rooted in our unshakeable confidence in God's character. We trust that God is love, his offer of love and relationship includes the whole world (1 John 4:8, John 3:16) and his desire is that no one should die without the opportunity to repent (2 Peter 3:9). The important thing to remind ourselves is that we are not God. We must not, and cannot, judge where anyone is at personally with God, nor should we presume that our salvation experience is what God requires of everyone else. As Christians we cling to and defend the biblical truth that Jesus is the only way to God, but also passionately trust that, based on God's great love and desire for humanity, there are as many different ways to Jesus as the people who come.

Michelle Tepper is an itinerant speaker for RZIM Europe and a guest lecturer at the Oxford Centre for Christian Apologetics (OCCA).

PREPARED TO GIVE AN ANSWER?

If you are looking for answers to the tough questions people ask, here are some resources to help you

Here's a sample of the wide range of books of Christian apologetics which are available. Some of these books cover the basics for anyone who wants to start thinking through issues – others will suit those who are looking for a more scholarly approach. Some are Christian classics – others are more recent publications. Your church or home group leader might be able to recommend a book best-suited to your needs.

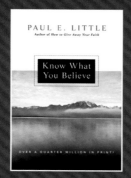

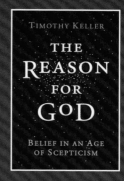

1. *The Evidence for the Resurrection* Norman Anderson (IVP)
2. *Is the New Testament Reliable?* Paul Barnett (IVP)
3. *The Historical Reliability of the Gospels* Craig Blomberg (Apollos)
4. *Blind Alley Beliefs* David Cook (IVP)
5. *The Evidence for Jesus* R T France (Regent College)
6. *It Makes Sense* Stephen Gaukroger (Scripture Union)
7. *What About Other Faiths* Martin Goldsmith (Hodder & Stoughton)
8. *You Must Be Joking- Popular Excuses for Avoiding Jesus Christ* Michael Green (Hodder & Stoughton)
9. *Searching Issues: Seven Significant Questions* Nicky Gumbel (Alpha International)
10. *The Reason for God: Belief in an Age of Scepticism* Timothy Keller (Hodder & Stoughton)
11. *Mere Christianity* C S Lewis (HarperCollins)
12. *Know What You Believe* Paul E Little (IVP)
13. *The Best of Josh McDowell - A Ready Defense* compiled by Bill Wilson (Thomas Nelson)
14. *Bridge Building - Effective Christian Apologetics* Alister McGrath (IVP)
15. *Cross-examined* Mark Meynell (IVP)
16. *Why Trust the Bible?: Answers to 10 Tough Questions* Amy Orr-Ewing (IVP)
17. *Trilogy: The God Who Is There, Escape from Reason, He Is There and He Is Not Silent* Francis Schaeffer (IVP)
18. *What's the Point?* Norman Warren (Lion)
19. *Why We Can't Believe* Paul Weston (IVP Frameworks)
20. *If God Then What?* Andrew Wilson (160 pages IVP)
21. *Simply Christian - Why Christianity Makes Sense* Tom Wright (SPCK)
22. *Lord Help My Unbelief - Re-examining 'The Case Against Christ'* John Young (BRF)
23. *Jesus The Verdict* John Young (Lion)
24. *Who Made God?: And Answers to Over 100 Other Tough Questions of Faith* Ravi Zacharias and Norman L Geisler (Zondervan)
25. *Why Jesus?: Rediscovering His Truth in an Age of Mass Marketed Spirituality* Dr Ravi Zacharias (Faithwords)

Apologetics websites
Bethinking- www.bethinking.org
Apologetics Index- www.apologeticsindex.org
Apologetics.com- www.apologetics.com
Christian Apologetics & Research Ministries- www.carm.org
Impact Apologetics- www.impactapologetics.com

10 HELPFUL REMINDERS

Our call is to open our mouths knowing that only he can open hearts, says Martin Durham

1 Knowing God first

'I am the vine; you are the branches. If a man remains in me and I in him, he will bear much fruit; apart from me you can do nothing' (John 15:5).

It is striking that the early church did not see evangelism as an activity. Rather it was a natural response to their faith in Christ. Whilst not complete, perhaps a helpful definition of evangelism is 'the overflow of our love for Jesus Christ'.

Intimacy with God is foundational. Spiritual disciplines are the doorway to intimacy. Are prayer, fasting, study of God's word, meditation, silence and solitude (to name some) part of your walk with God?

Challenge: Set goals to exercise spiritual disciplines.

2 Only God can change someone, not you

Preparing to share Jesus can be daunting. The truth that only God can change someone is liberating! We must remember, it is his work. Our call is to open our mouths knowing that only he can open hearts. The fruit belongs to him.

'The Lord opened her (Lydia's) heart to respond to Paul's message' (Acts 16:14).

Challenge: Read Acts 8:26-40, a picture of God's sovereignty and our call to share Jesus.

3 Pray for your friends

Prayer is integral to the believer's life. Prayer is easy to talk about, but often difficult in practice. How frequently does God find you on your knees in the secret place crying out to him for your friends who do not know him?

A powerful and inspiring image: '… holding… golden bowls full of incense, which are the prayers of the saints' (Revelation 5:8).

Challenge: Prayerfully list five friends whom you will commit to pray for daily.

4 Expect opportunities to arrive

Only by the power of the Holy Spirit can a heart be changed, and we have the amazing privilege of being his ambassadors to a lost world.

William Carey is attributed as saying, 'Attempt great things for God. Expect great things from God.' Expectation is powerful. It inspires action.

Do we have an intimacy with God that means we readily recognise the sound of his voice as he prompts us to witness? Do we believe he could use us today to change someone's life?

Challenge: See interruptions in your daily schedule as potential God opportunities. Ask God in that moment to open your spiritual eyes.

5 Talk about Jesus

'…they called them… and commanded them not to speak or teach at all in the name of Jesus' (Acts 4:18).

Lots of people talk about 'god' but the name of Jesus stands alone. We are told to call upon his name for salvation (Acts 2:21) as there is no other name by which we can be saved (Acts 4:12).

There is power in the name of Jesus. His name is scandalous to the world.

Challenge: 'What did you do at the weekend?' Answer this question in a way that talks about Jesus.

6 Avoid jargon

'Have you been washed in the blood of the Lamb?' It is important to consider how everyday Christian language can become jargon in the ears of the unbeliever.

How does the unbeliever understand 'sin', 'repentance', 'salvation' and 'being saved'? And what on earth does 'inviting Jesus into your heart' mean? Even the word 'Christian' can confuse people. Many identify themselves as 'Christian' because they were born in the UK and/or are a 'good person'.

Challenge: Take the words above and find new words to say the same thing.

7 Know when to stop – leave people hungry to know more

Resist the thought that says we must share the complete gospel message in every 'God conversation'.

Genuine interest is easily gauged through strong eye contact, questions being asked etc. When eyes start to wander or to glaze over, maybe it is time to stop, at least for now. You change the subject before they do. Remember, salvation is God's work.

Challenge: Pray for discernment when sharing Jesus, knowing when to stop.

8 Recognise that people are on a journey

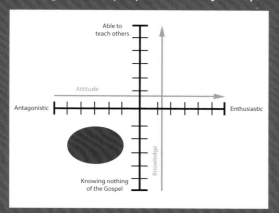

The circle in this diagram is where most people are. Fewer and fewer people seem to have any knowledge of the gospel, so they are more antagonistic to the message. The goal is to take people on the journey from the lower left quadrant to the upper right quadrant. The quadrant diagram emphasises that conversion to Christ is a process – evangelism moves people closer to Jesus.

Challenge: Listen to people. Which quadrant (stage of the journey) are they in? How can you help them take the next step on their journey of faith?

9 Build trust with people

Trust is in short supply. It is hard to gain and can be lost in a moment. Trust demands time. There are no short cuts to strong relationships. Consistency in friendship becomes important, therefore communicate regularly and demonstrate reliability. Practical assistance accelerates the building of trust. Be ready to minister to the needs of the person. Using someone's name, particularly early in a friendship, demonstrates that you care and builds bridges.

Challenge: Start to intentionally build a friendship with a neighbour.

10 Be prepared

'But in your hearts set apart Christ as Lord. Always be prepared to give an answer to everyone who asks you to give the reason for the hope that you have' (1 Peter 3:15).

Like intimacy with God, setting apart Christ as Lord in our heart is utterly foundational. From this depth of relationship our evangelistic desire, our readiness to witness, and our words flow. It is as we fix our eyes upon Jesus that our love and compassion grows for those who do not know him.

Challenge: Pray that God will give you a daily opportunity to share Jesus.

Martin Durham is an evangelist with Kerygma180 (K180) of which he is the founding director. www.k180.org

STEPS TO FOLLOWING JESUS

Laurence Singlehurst on five keys to help people who are making a commitment to follow Jesus

Understanding is key, so when leading someone to Jesus, it is important to ask a few questions. What do you think it means to be a Christian? Who do you think Jesus is? What might he have done for you and what would it mean for you to be a Christian? What change do you think there might be in your life if you made a step of faith? If the person doesn't understand, then encourage them to attend a course introducing the Christian faith or meet with them one-to-one to help them understand.

The second key is surrender. Conversion means we put God at the centre of our lives, not ourselves (2 Corinthians 5:15).

Thirdly, confession. 'If we confess our sins, he is faithful and just and will forgive us' (1 John 1:9). Encourage people to confess one thing that they know is not right, that they are doing or have done. Let the Holy Spirit and their conscience tell them what it is, then encourage them to continue a life of confession and to receive forgiveness.

Fourthly, repentance (Acts 2:38) and a 'renewed mind' (Romans 12:2) is key. A step of surrender leads to changed values. We seek to live God's way.

Lastly, becoming a Christian is about joining in, being a part of God's family, the church, and joining in God's purpose in transforming our world with his love and wisdom.

Laurence Singlehurst speaks regularly at major events, conferences and churches. He worked in Youth with a Mission from 1976 to 2003 and as National Director from 1990 to 2003. He is author of Sowing Reaping Keeping *(IVP) and* The Gospel Message Today – Language that Connects in Communicating the Gospel *(Grove) and is currently Director of Cell UK, and a member of the HOPE leadership team.*

HOW TO LEAD SOMEONE TO JESUS

Be ready… says Martin Durham

There is a beautiful phrase found in John 1:42. It talks of Andrew finding his brother Simon to tell him he had found Christ. The scripture simply says: 'He brought him to Jesus'.

As you take those next steps after engaging in a 'God conversation', be ready to bring the person to Jesus. Ultimately, the very nature of the gospel demands a decision. Allow the Holy Spirit to direct that opportunity.

Take a few moments to share the gospel message with the person, helping them to count the cost in making this decision. Ask if they have any questions. Lead them to a place of response, perhaps by offering to pray with them. Thinking carefully about the language you use, ask whether they see the need to be rescued from their self-centredness (sin) and the consequences that brings? Do they believe Jesus died and rose again that they might know life in all its fullness, now and eternally? Are they ready to turn around from going their own way and embrace his forgiveness? Are they ready to put Jesus in the driving seat of their life?

We must recognise that their understanding can be limited at this point of decision. We are called to make disciples, not converts. Whilst the 'sinner's prayer' is not found in the Bible per se, such profession of faith marks a clear decision, and is a helpful, significant marker on the spiritual journey.

Maybe the person will want to use their own words as they make their response to Jesus. Alternatively, you could use one of the following prayers.

Traditional

Dear Lord Jesus, I know that I am a sinner, and I ask for your forgiveness. I believe you died for my sins and rose from the dead. I turn from my sins and invite you to come into my heart and life. I want to trust and follow you as my Lord and Saviour. In your name. Amen.

Contemporary

Lord Jesus, I am sorry that I have been going my own way, so often ignoring you. Please forgive me. Thank you for rescuing me from the consequences of living for myself and rejecting you. I want you to be in the driving seat of my life. Help me to be the person you designed me to be. I ask this in Jesus' name. Amen.

Martin Durham is an evangelist with Kerygma180 (K180) of which he is the founding director. www.k180.org

FOLLOW-UP

If you are unable to follow-up an enquirer personally, because he or she lives too far away from you, for example, the following might be of help.

Contact for Christ is a nationwide Christian follow-up service that is able to link those enquiring about the Christian faith with a local Christian who can help them. CfC has over 800 'Contacts for Christ' in the UK and Ireland drawn from over 30 denominations and church groups. Find out more at www.deo-gloria.co.uk/cfc.php

CONCLUSION - JUST DO IT!

Expect God to use you, says Andy Frost

'Therefore go and make disciples...' were some of the final words Jesus shared with his rag tag bunch of followers. Some of them doubted, some of them were not very well educated, some of them had let Jesus down spectacularly... and yet they were all given the same opportunity to partner in sharing his life transforming message.

The message of Jesus is good news that too often we have lost the confidence to share. Having read this resource, you can see there are a variety of ways in which you can help introduce people to a relationship with God. All of us have a part to play whether we are shy or loud, young or old, new Christians or long-term believers.

We don't mind which ideas you adopt and which ideas you ignore, as long as you jump in afresh with God's great plan to allow all people to have the opportunity to know him.

Realistically, everyday there will be both opportunities and excuses. Today choose to look for those opportunities and get over those excuses, with an expectation that God will use you. By stepping up, you can become part of somebody else's story of coming to know Jesus. What an incredible privilege that is!

And as you share, remember that sharing your faith really is the first step. We are commissioned to make disciples, helping people not just to come to faith but to grow in faith too as they become part of God's people, the church. Partnering with God in making disciples is a long-term process... and it begins today by sharing Jesus!

Andy Frost is Director of Share Jesus International and Mission Director of Crossing London. He tweets @andythefrosty

FAST AND PRAY

The more seriously we approach prayer and fasting, the more serious the results we will experience in our missional journey. Let us pray and fast, taking control in the spiritual realm, that we might see a continuous transformation of souls in our communities and our nation for Jesus.

Pastor Agu Irukwu, Chair of the Executive Council of RCCG UK and Senior Pastor of Jesus House, London.